ST. JOHN OF THE CROSS

AND

DR. C.G. JUNG

BOOKS BY JAMES AND TYRA ARRAJ

A TOOL FOR UNDERSTANDING
HUMAN DIFFERENCES
How To Discover and Develop Your Type
According to Dr. C.G. Jung and Dr. William Sheldon
(Out of Print)

ST. JOHN OF THE CROSS AND DR. C.G. JUNG
Christian Mysticism in the Light of
Jungian Psychology

THE TREASURES OF SIMPLE LIVING
A Family's Search for a Simpler and
More Meaningful Life in the Middle of a Forest

A JUNGIAN PSYCHOLOGY RESOURCE GUIDE

TRACKING THE ELUSIVE HUMAN
Volume I
A Practical Guide to
C.G. Jung's Psychological Types
W.H. Sheldon's Body and Temperament Types
and Their Integration

Forthcoming:

TRACKING THE ELUSIVE HUMAN
Volume II

CHRISTIAN MYSTICISM IN THE LIGHT OF JUNGIAN PSYCHOLOGY

ST. JOHN OF THE CROSS AND DR. C. G. JUNG

JAMES ARRAJ

INNER GROWTH BOOKS

For ordering information on this and other titles write:
   Inner Growth Books
   Box 520
   Chiloquin, OR 97624

The author invites your comments through the above
address.

This book is printed on acid free paper.

47122

Library of Congress Cataloging in Publication Data

Arraj, James.
   St. John of the Cross and Dr. C.G. Jung.

   Bibliography: p.
   Includes index.
   1. John of the Cross, Saint, 1542-1591. 2. Jung, C.G.
(Carl Gustav), 1875-1961. 3. Christianity--Psychology--
History. I. Title. II. Title: Saint John of the Cross and Dr.
C.G. Jung.
BX4700.J7A8   1986   248.2'2   86-11315
ISBN 0-914073-02-8

TO JOSEPH REX PATCHETT

FOR SHARING HIS KNOWLEDGE AND LOVE

OF JOHN OF THE CROSS

CONTENTS

A SHORT ORIENTATION

Many current attempts to revitalize the life of prayer are inspired by either the writings of St. John of the Cross or the psychology of Dr. C.G. Jung. Both are excellent choices. Even better would be a program of renewal under their joint inspiration.

Yet such a program faces three serious challenges: theological misgivings about the compatibility of Jung's psychology with Christian belief, long-standing misinterpretations of St. John's doctrine on contemplation, and the need to clarify the relationship between Jung's process of individuation and contemplation.

Parts I and II are devoted to resolving these first two problems, while Part III gives a practical demonstration of the relationship between individuation and contemplation in St. John's life and writings and in a variety of contemporary spiritual problems.

Let me put it more concretely. I am enthusiastic about the prospect of using Jung and St. John as practical guides in the interior life. But when this enthusiasm begins to run away with me I see Victor White deep in conversation with Jung in the tower at Bollingen and their subsequent estrangement. Or I see Juan Falconi and Antonio Rojas in the Madrid of the late 1620's evoking the name of John of the Cross with the best of intentions to fuel a popular enthusiasm for contemplation, yet paving the road that led to a distrust of mysticism that has lingered to our own day.

Although these problems are serious and will force us to take a difficult journey through the thickets of epistemology and the history of spiritual life in the 17th century, I believe they are surmountable and will help lay foundations for a renewal of the life of prayer and a practical science of spiritual direction.

PART I

JUNG'S PSYCHOLOGY AND CHRISTIAN FAITH

CHAPTER 1

INDIVIDUATION

A Russian Olympic sailing champion once declared that his success lay in his ability to see the wind in the form of colors. If that were true and not simply a way to discomfit his rivals, it is not much stranger than the special gift of C.G. Jung. Jung could perceive things existing beyond the spectrum of ordinary awareness in a realm he called the unconscious. Just how visible this unconscious was to him was never fully apparent until the publication of his **Memories, Dreams, Reflections.** In it he says: "The difference between most people and myself is that for me the 'dividing walls' are transparent. That is my peculiarity."(1)

What we all experience as invisible psychic winds that strike our awareness in the form of feelings, fleeting premonitions and inexplicable attractions, Jung saw as vibrant images, and this ability plays a major role in his discovery and development of a natural science of the psyche. He struggled to produce a psychology which would encompass this shimmering interior world and try to come to grips with questions of meaning, religion, and God. A psychology like his shakes our sense of being experts about who we are and challenges us to a journey from ego-consciousness into the unconscious in order to find a deeper and truer self.(2)

C.G. JUNG

Carl Gustav Jung was born in Switzerland near Lake Constance in 1875. His father was a clergyman in the Swiss Reform Church, and his early childhood was deeply influenced not only by his religious upbringing but by powerful inner experiences. He developed a strong interest in the natural sciences, and decided to become a doctor, but just at the completion of his studies he discovered psychiatry and found in it a way to combine his scientific interests and his fascination with the inner world revealed to him in his youth.

Early in his professional career he became acquainted with Freud's work and went on to become a highly regarded member of the psychoanalytic movement. By 1913 he had grown away from Freud to such a degree that a break became inevitable. He plunged into his own interior world, and through it became aware that beyond consciousness there existed not only suppressed fragments from the world of the ego, but a realm that had universal and collective qualities. This confrontation eventually began to crystallize in his written works and led him to an extensive study of mythology, alchemy and religion. Jung's writings, which fill 18 volumes in his collected works, are technical and scientific elaborations of questions that arose in his own life and in the lives of his patients. These researches became deeply preoccupied with religious questions, for Jung discovered that many of his mature patients did not find a solution to the problems that brought them to the consulting room until they found what he, himself, felt constrained to call a religious meaning to life. This growing awareness of the function of religion in the over-all economy of the psyche led Jung to consider various aspects of Catholic dogma like the Trinity, the Assumption of the Blessed Virgin Mary, and the Mass.

THE PROCESS OF INDIVIDUATION

Jung's greatest achievement was to discover an inner movement towards psychic development which he called individuation. This movement, far from being a vague and random impulse towards growth, is a highly complex and organically articulated inner journey with a definite goal. Jung attempted to formulate a psychology that would do justice to the whole psyche. He saw that the ego which we tend to identify with the whole of ourselves is, in reality, just one aspect of a greater totality which is comprised of the ego and the unconscious. It is the relationship of these two realities which forms the basis of the dynamics of the psyche; if the ego is accentuated too much, the psyche is no less ill than when it is asserted too little. The journey to a proper balance between the ego and the unconscious is the process of individuation.

Jung found it contained a number of discernible stages. For example, the demands and expectations of society, as well as the natural talents and conscious dispositions of the individual, unite to form an image which he called the persona. The persona is the face or mask of the conscious personality that the world comes to see, and which the individual himself often accepts as who he is, and this most visible aspect of the personality becomes the representative of the whole. While this is a convenient, natural shorthand for dealing with people and our obligations in regard to them, if we identify our persona with our whole personality, difficulties are bound to arise. What society dislikes and what we dislike about ourselves becomes hidden and repressed and split off. The persona becomes balanced by a shadow of the unpleasant realities we refuse to admit exist in our personalities.

Another step in the inner journey is the discovery of the anima or a hidden femininity in a man, or animus, a hidden masculinity in a woman. Each of us contains within ourselves an image of the opposite sex which vitally effects how we deal with other people. Only by becoming aware of it and trying to relate to it can we channel and direct the influence it has on our lives.

The shadow, anima and animus are simply names that Jung gave to some of the different aspects of the basic process of realizing that the whole psyche is comprised of both ego and unconscious. This unconscious in its deepest sense or collective unconscious is the reservoir of what it means to be human in all its ramifications. It is the matrix of human possibilities, a shaper of human behavior, and the source of recurring patterns of images and behavior that spiral through history. The realities underlying these patterns Jung called archetypes. Archetypes are not innate ideas or images, but the unconscious psychic structures which manifest themselves through concrete images and actions. Jung posited them in an attempt to explain why similar thoughts, images, and activities are to be found in men who have no possible historical connection with each other. The figure of the anima, for example, appears in ancient myths and religions, as well as the dreams of modern men. While it takes different outer forms depending on time and culture, its inner core of meaning remains the same.

The end goal of this journey into the unconscious is to become more fully human, that is, to be related to the total psyche. As the journey goes on, the ego can no longer pretend that it is at the center of everything. It sees that vital parts of its very personality are not parts of the ego at all. It must yield to a new center which recognizes the needs of both the ego and the unconscious. Jung called this new center the self.

The recognition of this greater reality on the part of the ego is at the foundation of his understanding of the psychological meaning of religion. Not only does the ego see that it is just part of a larger whole, but it becomes aware that the unconscious precedes it and goes beyond it at every turn. The ego can no longer simply consult its limited desires and its one-sided understanding, but must develop an attitude of receptivity towards the unconscious. But this psychological sense of religion comes not only from this recognition of a reality that is bigger than the ego, but also from the feelings that come to the ego from its relationship to the unconscious. Contents of the unconscious, emerging in dreams or as projections on outer events, can evoke a feeling of numinosity: a combination of awe and deep satisfaction, as if one has finally discovered a vital part of oneself in the very act of relating to something greater.

JUNG AND CHRISTIAN DOCTRINE

On the practical plane Jung had discovered how crucial it was for the health of his patients to rediscover a religious point of view. This meant that the ego had to experience something beyond itself, and even submit itself to the healing powers that came from the unconscious. Thus, he could talk about a psychological cure of souls, and it was these practical considerations that fueled his interest in studying Christian dogma.

When Jung turned, late in his life, to a formal examination of certain points of Christian doctrine, it was as an extension of his previous studies of the basic process of individuation. It is not surprising, then, that he would select those points that would best illustrate how Christian doctrine embodies this psychological reality.

Towards the end of his own journey of exploration of the unconscious Jung had begun to spontaneously draw circular figures, and he instinctively felt that these drawings were important in his attempts to come to grips with the unconscious. Later he discovered similar motifs in the dreams and fantasies of his patients. At a certain point in their psychological development some sort of center appeared to be emerging in the form of a circle or square, crown, ball, four objects, etc. In 1928 when he was preoccupied with these questions, he received a Taoist alchemical treatise, **The Secret of the Golden Flower.** This helped him understand how universal the psychic process was, for it contained many of these same motifs.

Therefore, when Jung began to ponder the question of the Trinity, it was inevitable that he would pose the question of whether the Trinity as a psychological symbol, not as an object of faith, represented a deficient stage of psychic evolution which would have within itself an impulse towards fuller development. In essence, should the three become four, and thus be a better symbol of the self? It appeared to Jung that the image of Satan balanced the image of the all good triune God. In a similar fashion, the masculine Godhead needed to be complemented by a feminine principle. Jung greeted the proclamation of the dogma of the Assumption of the Blessed Virgin Mary into heaven with pleasure, for he felt it confirmed his own insight about the necessity of an evolution in the image of God.

The problem of evil also became subject matter for Jung's psychological approach. He felt that the doctrine of evil as the privation of good was not adequate from a psychological point of view. Evil in the psyche, he reasoned, was as real as good, and was necessary in order to define good itself. When Jung came to interpret the story of Job, he did so in terms of a deficient image of God that became more conscious in man. The god-image had to have room within itself for both good and evil. In all these cases Jung tried to make it clear that he was not presuming to talk about God Himself, but only the image of God as it exists in man. He was upset when theologians attacked him for reducing Christianity to a psychological process, and he made it clear that he did not presume to speak either as a philosopher or a theologian. Chapter Two explores this question at greater length.

THE CHRISTIAN CONTEXT OF THE DISCOVERY OF INDIVIDUATION

The story of Jung's inner life is not simply an interesting appendix to his written works. It makes a vital contribution to understanding how his psychology was created. The whole process of the discovery of individuation started with his personal experiences of the unconscious, and these experiences are crucial for understanding the Christian context in which Jung elaborated his psychology. Jung states, "My life is the story of the self-realization of the unconscious", but it is also the story of Jung's relations to the Christian world he grew up in.

Jung was raised in a world of formal institutional religion. Not only his father, but eight of his uncles as well, were clergymen, and so he was bound to experience the almost inevitable tension between the demands of formal religious practice and the limitations of human nature. But this kind of problem is common to many people who are exposed to the human workings of religious organizations. In Jung's case they appear to have been greatly accentuated by the religious problems of his father who was caught in a desperate struggle between his role as pastor and his personal doubts about Christianity. His father's solution was to try to believe blindly and to reject any thinking about these doubts, which he felt could lead him to succumb to them. This effort at blind belief tormented him, and the whole family suffered as a result. The gloom caused by his father's struggles was compounded by the serious problems that existed in his parents' marriage. Jung associated reliability and powerlessness with his father, and unreliability with his mother who had left the home for a period during his early years. Yet there was something about his mother that hinted to him of hidden mysteries.

It was in this atmosphere of tension with its heavy overtones of his father's inefficacious will to believe that Jung had a dream that played a large role in shaping his life. It occurred when he was three or four years old, and in the dream he had descended into an underground chamber where he saw an enormous phallus on a golden throne. In his dream his mother told him, "That is the man-eater." The effect of this dream was so powerful that: "Lord Jesus never became quite real for me, never quite acceptable, never quite lovable, for again and again I would think of his underground counterpart, a frightful revelation which had been accorded me without my seeking it."(3)

A world of nature, instinct, sexuality and emotion appears in compensation for the formal, dead Christianity that was destroying his father. About this same time Jung saw a Catholic priest in his cassock, and the sight terrified him. Several years later he peered into a Catholic Church and stumbled and cut himself. He had the feeling he had done something forbidden: "Jesuits - green curtain - secret of the man-eater...So that is the Catholic Church which has to do with Jesuits. It is their fault that I stumbled and screamed."(4) Catholicism, too, with its emphasis on mystery, symbol and ritual also represented this other side.

When Jung was eleven he suffered another powerful experience which built on these earlier ones and confirmed and extended them. He was in the Cathedral square and was struck by its beauty: "The world is beautiful and the Church is beautiful, and God made all this and sits above it far away in the blue sky on a golden throne and..."(5) And then he felt that some terrible thought was on the verge of breaking through, and that he could not give into it under the pain of committing an unforgivable sin. Finally, after days of torment, he knew he had to think this terrible thought, and he came to the conclusion that God, Himself, had placed him in this predicament and wished to test him in a personal way. Finally, Jung let the thought come: "God sits on His golden throne, high above the world - and from under the throne an enormous turd falls upon the sparkling new roof, shatters it, and breaks the walls of the Cathedral asunder."(6) This thought filled him with an unutterable bliss, and through it he felt he had learned the meaning of God's grace, but if this was an experience of God, then he somehow had to understand the strange nature of God, and this burdened his youth.

What is striking about Jung's early years is how firmly he clung to the central importance of these inner events. They were accompanied by very tangible visual imagery

for which he was gifted. He had a profound dislike for any
kind of reasoning that detached itself from his imagination. Mathematics was a torment to him for what appeared
to be its arbitrary and abstract qualities. Even drawing
was an impossibility when it did not engage his imagination.

These inner visions were, in his mind, immediate experiences of God, and he sought among his schoolmates and
the adults he came in contact with to find an echo of
them in order to relieve the isolation and loneliness that
they plunged him into. Unfortunately, there was no one
he could talk to. Again and again, while listening to his
father preach, or to the theological discussions of his
uncles, Jung would repeat to himself: "But what about the
secret? The secret is also the secret of grace. None of
you know anything about that."(7) He felt he knew by
experience what people were exhorted to believe in, and
they certainly didn't know anything about these mysteries
directly. Otherwise they never would have dared to talk
about God in public.

The contrast between the world of faith and church observance and his inner religious experiences grew even
sharper when his Holy Communion ceremony passed without any transformation taking place. Jung was growing up
living in two different worlds. The first world of his conscious ego, which he called his number one personality,
wanted to get on in the world and make something of itself. But there was also another world, a number two personality, that was connected with past centuries, nature,
and "God's world", to which "belonged everything superhuman - dazzling light, the darkness of the abyss, the cold
and impassivity of space and time, and the uncanny
grotesqueness of the irrational world of chance."(8) In this
world both nature and the devil were seen as creatures
of God, and so the ultimate responsibility for forcing Jung
to commit his "sin" and to learn the terrible secret about
the nature of God rested with God Himself. Possessed by
the secret, Jung understood that, "God was, for me at
least, one of the most certain and immediate of experiences."(9)

As Jung grew older, his number one personality was
attracted to science, while number two was inclined to
comparative religion and archeology. But neither was satisfactory by itself, for science lacked an answer to ques-

tions of meaning, while religion lacked empiricism. The process of adjustment between the number one and number two personalities was a foreshadowing of what Jung was to call individuation which would attempt to combine science and religion, and questions of meaning with empiricism.

But there was a very real distinction, even chasm, in Jung's mind, between his inner world of religion and theology. Theology was the focus of Jung's anger and contempt as he watched his father suffer and yet could not find a way to communicate what he felt were the saving graces he had received. "Theology had alienated my father and me from one another...I was shaken and outraged at once because I saw how hopelessly he was entrapped by the church and its theological thinking. God, Himself, had disavowed theology and the Church founded upon it."(10)

When Jung entered upon his university studies, he was attracted neither by theology nor by the prevailing scientific materialism. He found them both lacking from the point of view of his inner experience and what was already his favorite intellectual yardstick, Kant's **Critique.** His last-minute discovery of psychiatry allowed him to pursue a professional career without renouncing the interests of his number two personality. "Here was the empirical field common to biological and spiritual facts, which I had everywhere sought and nowhere found."(11)

With enormous single-mindedness Jung strove to master his psychiatric milieu, and his attraction to Freud and the psychoanalytic movement gave him a place in the world that suited the needs of his number one personality. Underlying, however, his university and psychiatric career were his inner religious experiences that were slowly gestating and waiting for the time when they could openly appear. When Jung broke with Freud and most of his psychoanalytic colleagues, he found himself at the midpoint of his life with family and profession, and even an international reputation, but with something vital missing. He could not articulate his own sense of the meaning of life, his own myth. He needed a way in which to break out of the confines of his conscious personality and find a new source of life. In order to overcome this impasse he turned to building miniature cities which had been a favored occupation of his childhood. He created a whole town out of little stones, and in it he built a church, but it was incomplete. One day he found a stone shaped like a four-sided pyramid, and he placed this as the altar of the church, and as he did so, he remembered his dream of the underground phallus with a sense of satisfaction.

Soon after, overcoming considerable resistances, he let himself go and began to see before his eyes strange scenes and people that lived in a world of the unconscious. He unleashed a vivid stream of images and fantasies, and exerted himself to the utmost to try to understand them and live out their implications for his life. He knew very well from his psychiatric work the dangers this involved, yet at the same time, he felt that if he did not personally undergo these experiences, he would be shirking his role as a healer of the psyche and he would never find his way to his own myth of meaning. His unique contribution to psychological science started with a personal submission to these experiences, an attempt at understanding them, and finally, a living out of their ethical implications day by day. Only then could he begin his scientific work in the more obvious sense of the word by attempting to establish the validity of these experiences for other people, and indeed, as universal psychological phenomena. Science was the way in which he could attempt to break out of the isolation and loneliness that these experiences had always caused him, for through it he could show that they were real, "and real not only as my personal experiences but as collective experiences which others also have."(12)

After he had been immersed for several years in the sea of the unconscious, he gradually began to find his bearings, and he drew a series of circular figures which he was later to call mandalas. The very act of drawing them seemed to help him gain some sort of balance. They helped him formulate the question of where these psychic experiences were leading. The very force and autonomy of these unconscious manifestations made him reluctant to try to artificially impose some sort of goal on them which would be a creation of the ego. He wanted to see the goal emerge out of the unconscious itself as a guarantee of its objectivity: "When I began drawing the mandalas, however, I saw that everything, all the paths I had been following, all the steps I had been taking, were leading back to a single point - namely, to the midpoint. It became increasingly plain to me that the mandala is the center. It is the exponent of all paths. It is the path to the center, to individuation."(13)

When Jung emerged from his confrontation with the unconscious he faced a lifetime of work in order to translate this interior experience into an objective scientific work which would be the creation of an empirical psychology that would describe this inner process of individuation. He was in a particularly difficult position of possessing his science in embryo in virtue of these experiences and his faculty of intuition, while at the same time facing the long and exacting process of articulating these insights in such a way that they could be understood by others. How difficult this task was to be can be illustrated by Jung's **Psychological Types**, which was his first major work after this period of inner psychic preoccupation. Though it was the fruit of many years of his own experience and those of his patients, it was criticized as if it were some theoretical conception that he had invented, a kind of intellectual parlor game.

Jung had stumbled upon what he felt to be the central process of human psychological development. But since the evidence was rooted in personal experience, he needed some way in order to circumvent the accusation that his work was simply a reflection of his own subjective limitations. In order to find this unimpeachable evidence of objectivity Jung turned to history, particularly the writings of the alchemists. In this rich but confusing welter of symbols he demonstrated that the alchemists had experienced the process of inner development that he had found in himself and in his patients: "I had very soon seen that analytical psychology coincided in a most curious way with alchemy. The experiences of the alchemists, were, in a sense, my experiences, and their world was my world."(14)

But the process of individuation was not the only parallel that existed between Jung and the alchemists. The alchemists, even though they often lived within Christendom and as faithful members of the Church, explored psychological realities through the medium of their chemical experiments, and these realities could be understood as compensations to the prevailing theological consciousness. Thus, Jung's explorations not only validated his premise of the universality of the individuation process, but they allowed him to carry on the interior debate he had taken up with theology in his youth.

Finally, when Jung in his mature years took up the

question of the Trinity, or commented on the Book of Job, he was doing so out of a lifelong preoccupation with the relationship that Christianity had with his psychology. There are two aspects in the history of Jung's thought that are so closely interwoven that it is only with the greatest difficulty that we can attempt to distinguish them. The first is Jung's crucial discovery of the process of individuation, and the second is how this discovery took shape in relationship to the Christianity that he grew up in. This Christianity became an immediate context and foil for his psychological work. While these two dimensions are profoundly united in Jung's life, it is still possible to see that they are distinct realities. An empirical exploration of the unconscious does not have an essential relationship with Christianity. A Jung, growing up with no religious background, or in another Christian tradition, or in another religious tradition altogether, could have conceivably made many of the same discoveries. In actual fact this, of course, did not happen, and so Jung's insights are in the setting of his Christian preoccupations, and thus Jung's understanding of and attitudes towards Christianity, as important as they may be in indicating some of the weaknesses of Christianity as it is actually lived today, do not have the same weight as his empirical discoveries, even though these discoveries from a concrete point of view might not have been realized by Jung except as compensations to the Christianity of his childhood. For example, Jung's discussions of trinity and quaternity, despite the value they might have for a theologian exploring the psychological dimensions of Trinitarian doctrine, are not essential to Jung's formulation of the process of individuation, but rather illustrative of it. Jung explored what could be called the natural religiosity of the psyche, and he asserted that in doing so he was not trying to act as a philosopher or theologian. Yet his writings often were seriously criticized by these people. It is time to examine this question more closely, for unless it is resolved, it will impede the use of Jung's psychology as an instrument in elaborating the Christian life of prayer.

CHAPTER 2

A TYPOLOGY OF THE SCIENCES

It is hard for us to comprehend the intensity and numinosity of Jung's psychological experiences; they were not half-glimpsed fragments of images that barely penetrated into the day-lit world, but rather, emotionally-laden visions with more force than everyday events. The gift of these inner experiences and the single-mindedness with which Jung pursued their meaning superbly equipped him to create a science of the psyche. In it he would try to explain these experiences which we all have, though in different degrees of intensity and accessibility.

A NATURAL SCIENCE OF THE PSYCHE

Jung started his scientific work on the basis of empirical facts, that is, these observable, inner psychological events. He experienced these facts in himself and his patients, and through his researches in myth and religion. Then in an attempt to understand these facts he organized them by means of a hypothesis which attempted to link them together under a heading that would best seem to explain them. The facts themselves were there for anyone to verify who had the opportunity to come in contact with this inner psychological world, and the interpretation of the facts could, and did, change as more material came to light and better explanations were framed in order to account for them. Jung found in his own dreams and those of his patients, and in his spontaneous drawings, images of circles, balls, crowns, gems, coins, etc., as we have seen. These were empirical facts. By observing how they appeared and in what context and how these symbols were transformed and what feelings were connected with them, he eventually concluded that they were all manifestations of one underlying factor, and he called this factor, or archetype, the self. The word self, however, was not meant to express a content that went beyond the initial material upon which it had been based. It was not an explanatory concept in the sense that it had an intrinsic meaning that extended further than the observable phenomena. "The name should mean to him (the psychologist) no more than a mere cipher, and his whole conceptual system should be to him no more than a trigonometrical survey of a certain geographical area in which the fixed points of reference are indispensible in practice, but irrelevant in theory."(1) It is the observable empirical material that holds the supremacy. If this material outstrips the organizing power of the hypothesis, then the hypothesis must be discarded and another one created. Whatever the self may be in itself is not the issue. The hypothesis is not attempting to go beyond the observable appearances and to discover the causes that give rise to them. It is content to grasp the underlying object through the network of observations, and by coordinating these observations understand something about the object, not directly, but through the creation of the hypothesis which serves as a substitute for the object. The hypothesis, then, is a construct, a descriptive vehicle, by which the empirical material can be dealt with. By its nature it is never complete and constantly evolves. Its value lies in its applicability to similar observations, and so in this sense it has an explanatory power. For example, many people will find in their dreams the same images and feelings that Jung grouped together under the concept of the self, and thus it will appear to them as a reasonable explanation of their own experience. Two mistakes must be avoided: the first is treating Jung's concepts as if they were things in themselves. "Functional concepts in psychology - and not only in psychology - do not denote things like a liver or a brain, but constellations of phenomena exhibiting a certain dynamic structure and conforming to certain laws...If the concept serves to describe and account for a well-defined group of phenomena clearly and economically, it is scientifically useful."(2) The second mistake is to separate Jung's concepts from the empirical material upon which they are based. This happens, for example, when Jung's ideas are criticized as if he simply thought them up by means of some kind of conscious ingenuity, and then tried to apply them to his patients.

Jung's psychology has a number of distinctive qualities. Although it is an empirical science, it is not an experimental one in the strict sense, for it does not artificially limit the possible factors that can give rise to a psychic response in order to test one portion of the psyche at a time. It attempts to be a science which listens to and observes the whole psyche, both conscious and unconscious, and thus it does not want to limit the answers that the psyche as a whole can give. However, to be non-experimental is not the same as being non-verifiable, for the results that it obtains can be verified by further observation. It attains the facts on which it bases itself not only by measurement, but principally by observation.

Jung's psychology could be called a science of man inasmuch as he is a psychic being; it is a vision of man constructed through observable psychic facts. These psychic images were at once at the very center of Jung's personal sense of identity and the life-blood out of which he created his psychology. When we understand this, we are in a position to grasp his tremendous passion for collecting more and more concrete material. Jung was attempting to understand the structure and dynamics of the whole psyche, and the only way he could do this was to surround himself with its manifestations, whether they came from himself or his patients or modern literature, ancient myths, religious doctrines, etc. All these fields were fertile hunting grounds for him inasmuch as their contents existed in the psyche of man. He repeated many times that even if a field itself had no intrinsic truth, it still had a psychic reality inasmuch as it existed in the human psyche. The more material he could assimilate, the wider empirical base he would have for erecting his theoretical constructs, with the promise that having seen the phenomena in all its facets his hypothesis would be as well grounded as possible. Jung moved from empirical material to hypothesis and back again in a ceaseless quest to deepen the foundation of his psychology. He spent years, for example, trying to decipher the symbols of the alchemists until he had reduced their mass of material to simple form. In **Mysterium Coniunctionis:** "if one examines the original draft of the work, one discovers, incredibly enough, that by itself it would have made a relatively short book: a nucleus of basic concepts tied together logically, in the form of a hypothetical construct."(3)

Then he reclothed these hypotheses in their full empirical regalia so that they would appear to the scientific
public in their integral form.

JUNG AND KANT

Jung always felt an affinity for Kant's philosophy, and
cited it on many occasions. Yet, if we give this attraction
a philosophical meaning we can be led into many difficulties. Jung was not a philosopher, not even a Kantian one.
What he found in Kant was a philosophical echo of his own
distinctive psychological point of view, for in many ways
Kantian philosophy is constructed after the pattern of
empirical science rather than that of traditional metaphysics. Jung's choice of Kant was more instinctive than deliberate, for Kant was the methodology of science raised
to the level of philosophy. For Jung, Kant was the way
to ward off his two principle adversaries: a 19th century
science embedded in a matrix of materialism and rational-
ism, and the world of philosophers and theologians who
could see no connection between the world of the psyche
and the realms they laid claim to. When Kant said that
the extra-mental thing in itself was unknowable, this coincided with Jung's perception that the thing behind the
phenomena was not his goal, and when Kant said that the
perceptions we received from things are organized by the
categories that exist in our mind, Jung saw in this a confirmation of the role of the archetypes in shaping psychic
phenomena. Thus, Kant confirmed Jung's deepest inclination
to put the psychic image before the thing in itself and to
see that these images were reflections of the underlying
unknowable realities. Both as a man and a scientist, Jung
wanted nothing more than to be free to pursue this way
of psychic images. Let his critics, he seems to say, fight
with Kant and leave him in peace to pursue his work.

If we criticize Jung as if he were a philosopher, or as
if he deliberately studied Kant in order to clarify the
epistemological foundations of his psychology, we will be
at a loss to understand the import of his use of Kant. In
virtue of Jung's method, he could not know the thing in
itself, he could only know it through psychic phenomena.
Thus, on the one hand he talks of the self being a limiting
concept whose content is unknown to us, or how "the

archetype in itself is empty and purely formal, nothing but a facultas praeformandi."(4) At the same time, Jung never doubted that the psychic phenomena actually manifested the archetypes, that he was knowing the archetypes through the phenomena. If we turn Jung into a philosopher, we will be led to say that he is making the archetypes unknowable and, at the same time, claiming to know them through the psychic images and emotions. Then we will urge him to find a more coherent philosophical position.(5) Yet this problem will resolve itself if we allow Jung to be an empirical scientist who, though he is convinced that the object of his science is not the thing in itself, is implicitly realistic. He realizes there is something, some unknowable, grounding his observations. "In my effort to depict the limitations of the psyche, I do not mean to imply that **only** the psyche exists. It is merely that, so far as perception and cognition are concerned, we cannot see beyond the psyche. Science is tacitly convinced that a non-psychic transcendental object exists."(6)

If we understand this statement from the point of view of Jung's empirical science of the psyche, it expresses the fact that the material the scientist is in contact with, the psychological facts, are looked at as manifesting the non-psychic object that cannot be known directly. Jung goes on: "...I have never been inclined to think that our senses were capable of perceiving all forms of being. I have therefore even hazarded the postulate that the phenomenon of archetypal configurations - which are psychic events **par excellance** - may be founded on a **psychoid** base, that is, upon an only partially psychic and possibly altogether different form of being. For lack of empirical data, I have neither knowledge nor understanding of such forms of being which are commonly called spiritual."(7)

In short, the scientist is convinced that he is dealing with real things, the extra-mental objects, as it were, but he is equally convinced that they remain unknowable in themselves and are only known through the psychological phenomena that manifest them.

Jung maintained this distinctive scientific viewpoint even when he was talking about God. He often distinguished between talking about the god-image which was in the province of the psychologist, and talking about God as if God were a direct object of cognition. He never identified God with the unconscious from an objective point of view since both these things were unknowable in themselves to the psychologist, and therefore could not be compared to each other according to their inner natures. At the same time, from the point of view of psychological experience or subjectivity, he felt there was no way to distinguish between the experience of God and the experience of the unconscious. From the perspective of the subjective experience itself, the use of the term God becomes synonymous with the use of the term unconscious. Yet Jung realized that the term God recognizes another psychological note by which we give expression to the peculiar way in which we experience the workings of these autonomous concepts. "The great advantage of the concepts "Daimon" and "God" lies in making possible a much better objectification of the **vis-à-vis**, namely a **personification** of it."(8).

JUNG, PHILOSOPHY AND THEOLOGY

If Jung was acting as an empirical scientist, why did he have so many difficulties with people who held philosophical and theological points of view? There are a number of reasons why the dialogue between Jung's psychology and theology has been much less fruitful than it could have been. First, there is the newness of a natural science of the psychology that tries to account for the whole psyche. Both the contents and the methodology are strange to philosophers and theologians, who often lack the grounding in empirical experience that is vital in understanding Jung's formulations. Secondly, there is the inclination of philosophically-minded people to find an explicit philosophy in Jung. Finally, there is something in Jung's presentation of his scientific position that hinders communication between his psychology and theology.

The very gift Jung possessed which enabled him to be so sensitive to the unconscious also led him to identify his personal point of view with his scientific one. His personal way of seeing coincided with the nature and limits of his scientific methodology. It was not as if his views on science were one thing and his views on religion another. When he used the terms philosophy or theology or metaphysics, he tended to identify them with each other and use them not only to describe the area that lay outside of science, but also lay beyond the possibility of any sure knowledge. He unconsciously tended to identify his scientific methodology with Kant's **Critique,** and then use them both as a kind of measure to indicate that theology did not really know the things it purported to. Theology in his mind understood neither epistemology nor experience. He had listened to the theological discussions of his uncles and experienced the problems of his father, and felt that their belief was a blind as that of the materialists: "I felt more certain than ever that both lacked epistemological criticism as well as experience...The arch sin of faith, it seemed to me, was that it forestalled experience."(9) But experience here meant the kind of experiences that Jung went through himself and which were crucial in formulating his scientific method, while epistemology meant accepting the unknowability of the thing in itself.

There are many statements in Jung's writings that can be given two distinct interpretations: one as an expression of his scientific method, and the other as an extension of this method so that it becomes a judgment on the possibility of other ways of knowing.

"When I do use such mythic language, I am aware that "mana", "daimon", and "God" are synonyms for the unconscious - that is to say, we know just as much or just as little about them as about the latter. People only **believe** they know much more about them - and for certain purposes that belief is far more useful and effective than a scientific concept."(10)

"For lack of empirical data I have neither knowledge nor understanding of such forms of being which are commonly called spiritual. From the point of view of science it is immaterial what I may **believe** on that score, and I must accept my ignorance...All comprehension and all that is comprehended is in itself psychic, and to that extent we are hopelessly cooped up in an exclusively psychic world."(11)

Passages like these have an inner tendency to go beyond a statement of the scientific method and move towards a position about the nature of knowledge itself. Belief, in Jung's mind, was the antithesis of knowledge, despite what other ends it might serve. His discussions with his father often ended with his father saying, "Oh, nonsense...you always want to think. One ought not to think but believe", and Jung would think, "No, one must experience and know."(12)

Later, when Jung examined statements about God found

in Indian religion, he makes what he feels to be a telling point against their simplicity. "The Indian lacks the epistemological standpoint just as much as our own religious language does. He is still 'pre-Kantian'."(13) Despite the language of these passages, Jung is not trying to be a philosopher, but since he lived so completely within the perspective of his own methodology, it was not comprehensible to him that people could take philosophy, faith and theology as ways of knowing. The issue at this point is not whether Jung in his evaluation of philosophy and theology is correct or not, but simply that he has inadvertently moved into the territory of epistemology. Philosophy and theology lay claim to their own distinctive facts and methodologies and ways of finding the truth, just like psychology does, and psychology is not the judge of these claims.

There is, then, a certain implicit philosophical position in Jung's psychology, a dimension of Kantian presuppositions, an epistemological position. This should not make us demand that Jung ought to have been a philosopher, and more importantly, it should not lead us to think that these philosophical presuppositions vitally distorted Jung's basic formulations. At the same time, we have to be aware of this aspect in Jung's writings, especially when it is a question of his interpretations of Christianity.

Jung interpreted Christianity after the pattern of his own psychology, and while, as I have maintained, there is a great value to Jung's empirical psychology, and even to his insights about the deficiencies and weaknesses of Christian theology, Jung's appreciation of Christianity never goes beyond this perspective, and unfortunately, tends to assert that it is not possible to go beyond this perspective.

Jung's psychology has been accused of being a Jungian religion, and a new version of Christianity. This is false inasmuch as analytical psychology is an empirical science, and the religious object in itself falls outside of its competence. It is religious inasmuch as it examines the religious function in man and its manifestations, but this form of religiosity does not extend beyond the bounds of empirical science, and does not constitute the formulation of a religion. The accusation does, however, hit upon the epistemological ambiguity that I have been examining. Analytical psychology lays itself open to the charge of creating a religion to the degree it finds insuperable, universal, epistemological barriers which deprive religion of any distinctive and genuine kind of knowing; if the possibility of knowing the religious object is denied, then what is left to religion is the religious function, and therefore Jung's psychology can function as a religion just as well as anything else.

Christian theology cannot admit the validity of this approach without suffering the loss of its own distinctive nature and method. There is no theology in Jung that can be transposed into an authentic Christian context as a direct development of traditional theology or as a replacement for it. Jung's highly provocative comments on the trinity and quaternity and the nature of evil and the role it should play in the god-image are not theology and should not be taken as theology. These ideas can be of great value to the theologian who will have the courage to use them to help purify the human dimension of his theological formulations, but at the same time, he cannot allow them to displace the content of these formulations. Even though Jung's empirical psychology grew and was formulated within the context of a certain kind of appreciation of Christianity, it is formally distinct from this context, and the use of Jung's psychology does not demand the acceptance of his interpretation of Christianity.

This is not the place to attempt to justify the validity of metaphysics, faith and theology as ways of knowing. It is important, however, to realize that a more nuanced epistemology could appreciate Jung's scientific methodology without, at the same time, feeling compelled to negate these other areas.

JACQUES MARITAIN AND THE PHILOSOPHY OF NATURE

Jacques Maritain, 1882-1973, was born in Paris and was studying philosophy at the Sorbonne with his wife Raissa when they were both converted to Catholicism. Maritain went on to become one of the leading figures in the revitalization of the philosophy of St. Thomas Aquinas. He combined a remarkable grasp of Thomistic philosophy with a deep interest in contemporary events. He wrote extensively on metaphysics, the creative processes of art and poetry, and the social implications of Thomism. Less

known, but equally important, are his writings on the epistemology of the modern sciences and his attempts to lay
the groundwork for the rejuvenation of the philosophy of
nature.

Unfortunately, despite being contemporaries, Jung and
Maritain seemed to have been almost completely unaware
of each other's works. The closest their paths crossed was
Maritain's Mellon lectures which were published as **Creative Intuition in Art and Poetry** by Bollingen, and contained some scattered footnotes on Jung's ideas.

The Degrees of Knowledge, published in 1932, represents one of Maritain's finest achievements. It was an
attempt to formulate an epistemological topography, as it
were, that would recognize the distinctive methods of the
modern sciences and of philosophy and theology, and yet
bring them into relationship with each other. A central
role in this synthesis was assigned to the philosophy of
nature, which could be called a philosophical understanding
of physical reality. In ancient and medieval times there
were no empirical sciences, or sciences of phenomena as
we know them now. The very methodology proper to the
sciences themselves remained implicit and overshadowed
by the deductive and ontological mode of proceding of the
philosophy of nature with its talk about matter and form,
body and soul, etc. As the empirical sciences grew in
strength and in an implicit awareness of their own methodologies, they felt constrained to revolt against philosophy,
and especially the philosophy of nature, that had dominated
the field of the physical real for so long. This split between philosophy and the sciences had unfortunate consequences for both. The once robust discipline of the philosophy of nature wasted away. It tended to be more and
more cut off from the life-giving contact with physical
reality and replace this contact with empty speculation.
The sciences, for their part, became involved with various
pseudophilosophies like mechanism and a scientific materialism which Jung felt constrained to struggle against. In
the 20th century the sciences became conscious of their
own methods and their limitations, and were led, in many
cases, to the borders of metaphysics.(14) Yet, between the
sciences and philosophy, there was a great chasm, and in
Maritain's mind the most satisfactory way to bridge it was
an exact understanding of the methods of the modern
sciences and a renewal of the philosophy of nature. The

philosophy of nature, while being closely related to metaphysics, studied the physical world and thus was best suited to mediate between the empirical sciences and metaphysics.

This bridge-building has, in fact, been going very slowly. It is hard for the modern, scientifically trained mind, even when it is aware of the limitations of the scientific method, to credit philosophy as a genuine way of knowing. The very palpability of psychological facts that founds and governs an empirical psychology like Jung's becomes a habit of mind that makes it difficult to appreciate what Maritain called the poverty and majesty of metaphysics which extends to the philosophy of nature as well. They are poor in their very relationship to sensible matter which is at the heart of the experimental sciences, while they are rich in far-reaching insights that allow a glimpse of the central realities of human existence. While metaphysics, for example, is based on facts, these facts, far from being acquired by elaborate equipment or subtle or complicated research, are very simple, e.g., the fact that things exist and the fact that different kinds of things exist, etc. The very simplicity of these facts can make them suspect in modern eyes, and the proper employment of these simple facts demands a certain kind of metaphysical intuition.(15)

From the other side, the philosophy of nature that Maritain envisioned is still groping to find its proper relationship between the world of metaphysics and the actual practice of the modern sciences. It can be tempted in either direction: to withdraw into a world of philosophy, leaving the actual exploration of the physical real to the sciences, or it can lose sight of its own distinctive methodology and become a pseudophilosophy that merely imitates the methods and findings of modern science. Despite all these limitations and difficulties, it is valuable to situate Jung's psychology within Maritain's schema of epistemological types. This will allow us to see that the adventitious philosophical presuppositions in Jung's formulation of his psychology are not irremediable obstacles to the use of his psychology as a tool of theological understanding.

THE EMPIRICAL SCIENCES

Science means today the empirical sciences, and Mari-

tain coined the word empiriological to distinguish them
clearly from the philosophy of nature. As Jung indicated,
the sciences today are not looking for any knowledge of
things in themselves. Maritain states, "...the possibility of
observation and measurement replaces the essence or quid-
dity which philosophy seeks in things."(16) As we have
seen, Jung felt there was something underlying the phenomena, but this something could not become the object of
scrutiny of his science. He grasped that "something" indirectly through his observations.

Maritain divided the empiriological sciences into two
broad categories: the empiriometrical and the empirioschematic. The empiriometrical "are materially physical and
formally mathematical", that is, they studied the sensible
or physical real from the point of view of mathematics
and its laws. Modern physics is the chief example of an
empiriometrical science. It starts from the physical world
in as far as it is measurable, and submits this data to the
world of mathematics and, finally, checks its conclusions,
again in relationship to what is measurable. The empirioschematic sciences, on the other hand, deal with observable aspects of the physical real more than with measurable ones, and they create their hypotheses on the basis
of these observations and verify them by means of further
observation. Biology and psychology tend towards the empirioschematic type of science, and Jung's psychology is
best viewed as one of these empirioschematic sciences.

There has been a certain amount of tension between
a psychology that has been conceived empiriometrically and
Jung's empirioschematic psychology, and I have touched
on this question in relationship to psychological types elsewhere.(17) Both psychological sciences can cover the same
subject matter, but each in its distinctive fashion. This
does not mean, however, they will reach identical conclusions, exhibit the same degree of competence or undergo
the same attractions. When properly employed, they com-
plement each other, yet because of the very nature of
biology and psychology, the empirioschematic approach will
go further than the empiriometrical one. As Jung puts it:
"...the more we turn from spacial phenomena to the non-
spaciality of the psyche, the more impossible it becomes
to determine anything by exact measurements."(18) Maritain expresses basically this same point of view: "...as one
rises above the world proper to physics, and as the object

gains in ontological richness and perfection, the quantitative aspect of the behavior under consideration becomes, not less real, but less significant and more subordinate, and the science in question less reducible to an interpretation which looks solely to mathematics for its form and laws."(19)

If there has been difficulty among empirical psychologists because of the diversity of methods employed, this difficulty is small when compared to trying to bring together an empirical psychology and a philosophical psychology such as exists as part of a philosophy of nature. Here, again, two psychologies are looking at the same things, but under different aspects. The empirioschematic psychology sees "a stream of sense appearances stabilized by a center of intelligibility", while the philosophical psychology sees "an intelligible object expressing itself through a stream of sense appearances".(20) Jung's psychology is dealing with sensible being, but as observable, while the philosophy of nature "deals with sensible being, but deals with it first and foremost as intelligible".(21) This philosophical psychology is built upon philosophical facts, but instead of these facts leading to hypotheses to be verified in terms of the observable, they lead towards the intelligible center or essence of things, though it rarely attains this essence with any clarity.

A psychologist with an empirioschematic approach like Jung's can find himself in a difficult position. While he is attracted by modern physics and berated by his empiriometrically-oriented colleagues for his unscientific approach, he sees no way in which he can quantify his most important psychological conceptions. He can't subordinate his psychology to the language of mathematics. At the same time, the very nature of his observations and his work with people suffering from a lack of meaning leads him to formulate concepts like archetype and self, while his scientific methods precludes his knowing these things in themselves. Further, as was the case with Jung, his implicit philosophical presuppositions led him toward the unsubstantiated conclusion that no knowledge of things in themselves is possible under any method. The empirioschematic psychologist or biologist, by the very nature of the subject matter of their science, will be led to ask "metaphenomenal questions to which they might try to reply with their own conceptual equipment and their proper

methods of analysis; then they will obtain in most favorable cases and by indirect paths and the delimitation of
unknowns solutions that resemble philosophical solutions and
are tangential to them".(22) This process is illustrated in
Jung's work by his formulation of the concept of the self
or the psychoid foundation of phenomena. Just as there
is an implicit realism in Jung's work, there is an implicit
attraction towards the philosophy of nature, and the inverse is true as well. The philosophy of nature is attracted
to an empirical psychology that will be broad enough and
daring enough to view the psyche or soul as a whole from
the point of view of phenomena while it itself tries to
view it from the aspect of essence or intelligible center,
that is, attempts to answer the question of what the soul
is in itself.

The attraction of Jung's psychology to philosophy, even
if it became explicit, would not at all dilute the autonomous vocabulary and methodology of this psychology.
Philosophical ideas or methods coming from a philosophical
psychology could not enter into the actual constitution of
an empirical science. Yet the principles coming from the
philosophy of nature could act "as regulative principles,
as directive principles, orienting thought and research, but
not entering into the very structure of these sciences
themselves."(23) Jung's psychology is burdened with a philosophical position even though he did not wish to philosophize. He did not have to philosophize in order to carry
out his scientific activity, yet out of the awareness of the
validity of his own method he doubted the validity of the
methods of philosophy and theology. This left him with the
enormous task of trying to reconstruct from the point of
view of his own methodology the realities and questions
that were once dealt with by these other disciplines. We
have to recognize the possibility that there can be a difference between a psychological treatment of these realities, which was the gift of his method, and the need to
reinterpret these realities that sprang from Jung's belief
that philosophy and theology had no sure way of knowing,
no way of doing science. Just as there is no need to deny
the validity of an empirioschematic psychology in order
to justify an empiriometric one, there is no need to deny
the possibility and existence of a philosophical psychology
in order to protect the autonomy of an empirioschematic
psychology. It is at the very limits or boundaries, the

interface of psychology and theology, where Jung's psychology is led to make its boldest assertions and its most sweeping hypotheses, and it is here that it would benefit from the climate created by an authentic philosophy of nature. It could then realize, though not in the proper texture of its conceptual lexicon, the fittingness of its own concepts which are empiriological reflections of realities that can also be viewed from the ontological point of view. It would be relieved of the burden of an idealistic philosophy that tends to close it in upon itself and negate the currents of realism that run through all genuine scientific activity.

There are several aspects of Jung's psychology which can be interpreted as showing the effects of this effort of reinterpretation. First of all, it feels a certain attraction to modern physics, especially microphysics. Yet this attraction remains largely inefficacious because of the distinctive differences of method between Jung's psychology and mathematical physics. Both the psychologist and the physicist can agree that each, in his own way, is being led to the borders of metaphysics. The assertion that there is an archetypal foundation to both is an expression of their convergence towards metaphysics. Yet this convergence does not rest on any unity of methodology, but rather on the role metaphysics could play in the unification of the ways of knowing. Unfortunately, as we have said, there are many reasons why the scientist will not accept the possibility of there being a genuine metaphysics, and the idea that a philosophy of nature is a more suitable companion for Jungian psychology than physics remains unthinkable.

To take another example, Jung's explorations in alchemy served a genuine role in the validation of his hypothesis about the central role of the process of individuation in the economy of the psyche. There is, however, another way in which Jung's strong attraction for alchemy can be viewed. From the point of view of his own methodology the phenomena could never fully grasp the archetype. There remained, then, a hunger for a deeper and fuller contact that could only be assuaged, and only momentarily, by more and more examples and manifestations of the underlying archetypal reality. In short, there may well be in Jung's historical explorations of alchemy an element of inefficacious desire to explore the foundations of the archetypes in themselves. This seems to be the best explanation of Jung's statement about his culminating work on alchemy:

"In **Mysterium Coniunctionis** my psychology was at last given its place in reality and established upon its historical foundations. Thus my task was finished, my work done, and now it can stand. The moment I touched bottom, I reached the bounds of scientific understanding, the transcendental, the nature of the archetype per se, concerning which no further scientific statements can be made."(24)

Another example of this proliferation of the empirio-schematic method at the very frontier between empirical psychology and philosophical psychology can be found in Jung's reflections about life after death. He recognized that there was a hunger in men for certain kinds of knowledge like that dealing with the question of life after death that outstripped the resources of the methodology of his psychology. Jung accepted this as a legitimate human need, but since the epistemological limitations inherent in his science were accepted by him as the personal limits of his own knowledge, he could not turn to philosophy or theology to try to formulate an answer, while his instinctive realism and profound contact with the psyche urged him to address these questions anyway. And so he looked to dreams and myths in order to form some conception of life after death. It is as if he had explored his psychological science to its limits, but now was constrained to try to exceed these limits because of the importance of these questions that fall outside the scope of his science. What he did was accumulate the hints that entered his own domain and framed a hypothesis which remained unprovable. His reflections on life after death are an application of the models that prove efficacious in terms of the exploration of the unconscious, projected into the realm of the dead; Jung is speaking again of the basic process of individuation, but extending it further and further since there was no philosophy or theology he could collaborate with.

FR. VICTOR WHITE

The question of the relationship of Jung's psychology to the philosophy of nature which we have looked at from the epistemological point of view should not lead us to believe that such theoretical discussions are without practical ramifications. Many of the same issues surfaced in the relationship between Dr. Jung and Fr. Victor White, who made the first serious attempt to start building the bridge that would overcome the chasm between Thomistic philosophy and Jung's psychology. Their relationship, then, becomes a paradigm of the problems that beset the use of Jung's psychology within the context of Christian theology, and the difficulties in which their relationship fell serve as a warning to a too facile amalgamation of these two disciplines.

When late in life Jung turned to an intensive study of Catholic dogma, he very much wanted to have a Catholic theologian as a companion and colleague in the exploration of the relationship between his psychology and Catholic theology. The man who appeared on the scene at the opportune moment was Victor White, a Dominican priest with an excellent background in Thomistic philosophy and theology, and a keen interest in Jung's psychology. Before he had come in direct contact with Jung he had been part of a group of psychotherapists and clergy who had met at Oxford under the leadership of John Layard.(25) It was to this group that White addressed his first paper on Jung's psychology entitled **On the Frontiers of Theology and Psychology,** and it was under Layard who was a Jungian psychotherapist that he gained some practical experience of Jung's psychology. Victor White combined a genuine sympathy for Jung's psychology with a firm grasp of scholastic philosophy and theology and an awareness of how beneficial it would be to bring the two together. In September, 1945, he sent Jung some copies of his first publications in this area. At the time Jung was 70 years old and about to embark on his most important writings on Christianity, e.g., his study on the Trinity, and the **Answer to Job,** while Fr. White had written his initial article three years previously at age 40, that crucial time of new beginnings.

Jung's response was untypically warm and extensive. He wrote: "You are the only theologian I know of who has really understood something of what the problem of psychology in our present world means. You have seen its enormous implications. I cannot tell you how glad I am that I know a man, a theologian, who is conscientious enough to weigh my opinions on the basis of a careful study of my writings!"(26)

Even if we read into this a certain extension of cour-
tesies, there is much more involved here; Jung had a
genuine desire for contact with Catholic theology, but he
needed a theologian who could appreciate the nature of
his psychology. "As a rule they are astonishingly innocent
of actual psychological experience..." and he goes on to
say, "I envy you and all those enjoying full possession of
Scholastic philosophy and I would surely be among the first
to welcome an explicit attempt to integrate the findings
of psychology into the ecclesiastical doctrine."(27) Jung
ends this letter, "Well - a long letter! Not my style at
all. "It" has made an exception in your case, my dear
Father, because "it" has appreciated your conscientious and
farsighted work."(28)

Fr. White decided to visit Jung in the summer of 1946,
and Jung invited him to stay with him at his "little country place". This was Jung's tower at Bollingen that was
connected with his inner work, and to bring Victor White
there was to extend a special invitation to intimacy.

The visit touched them both deeply. Jung had "all sorts
of feelings or "hunches" about Fr. White (29) who, for his
part, recounted a dream "in which he was sailing with
Jung at the helm, from Norway to England. They were
passing through perilous rocks at great speed, but ' there
was no feeling of fear "because the wind was taking care
of us."(30)

Jung summed up the new level of their relationship:
"We are indeed on an adventurous and dangerous journey!"
(31) As Fr. White's dream indicates, he had embarked on
a journey into the unconscious, and this was to entail a
serious struggle to attempt to bring this psychological
experience into line with his theological understanding. At
the same time, Jung was undergoing the inverse process,
that is, to bring his psychological understanding into relationship with theology. Towards the end of this letter he
says, "Presently I must make up my mind to tackle my
dangerous paper about the psychology of the H. Trinity."
(32) This must have been a difficult decision and a strain
on both his body and psyche. Less than two weeks later
he suffered a serious heart attack.

The joint process of exploration continued over the
next several years, with both men recounting their dreams.
Some of the material, for example, in Jung's letters, was

not to appear in full form until **Memories, Dreams, Reflections.** Jung was resolutely moving ahead and articulating his thoughts on Christianity. These years saw the writing of his expanded version of his paper on the Holy Trinity, **Aion,** and finally, the **Answer to Job,** and Fr. White's paper on Gnosticism stimulated Jung to ask, "Have I faith or a faith or not?"(33) His answer is important, for from it we can gauge what this process of drawing psychology and theology together meant for him:

"I have always been unable to produce faith and I have tried so hard that I finally did not know anymore what faith is or means. I owe it to your paper that I have now apparently an answer: faith or the equivalent of faith for me is what I would call respect."(34)

This respect is an "involuntary assumption" for Jung because there is something to dogmatic truth that induces it in him, even though he doesn't understand it, and his life has been an attempt to understand what others can apparently believe. But if there is something about Christian truth that causes this respect, there is something about Buddhism and Taoism that brings it about as well.

Even though Jung had to overcome strong resistances in order to express his feelings about Christianity, when he expressed himself it was not in any radically new fashion, but rather, the articulation of insights that had preoccupied him his whole life, and now had reached mature form. His relationship with Fr. White, while it might have been a minor catalyst, does not seem to have added any new content to Jung's religious views.

While Jung was forging ahead, Victor White began to face mounting difficulties. The precise nature of these difficulties is hard to determine without the publication of his letters, and with the deletions that exist in Jung's letters to him. Apparently Fr. White was beset by a feeling of isolation which resulted from his growing psychological perception in an ecclesiastical atmosphere that had little appreciation of it. But undoubtedly the problem went deeper than this. White's reconciliation of his priestly and psychological roles was not simply a matter of his external position in the Church, but the problem was a personal one as well: could he reconcile Jung's religious ideas that he was getting more and more conversant with and involved in with his Catholic faith? These interior difficulties began to crystallize around the problem of evil, the privatio boni. Towards the end of 1949, in a review of what was to become a section of **Aion,** he criticized Jung's "quasi-Manichean dualism" and his "somewhat confused and confusing pages" in relationship to the privatio boni.

Jung's response was uncharacteristically mild, and he went so far as to footnote White's criticisms in the text of **Aion,** calling him "my learned friend". In a letter of response, he attempts to clarify the problem:

"The question of Good and Evil, so far as I am concerned with it, has nothing to do with metaphysics; it is only a concern of psychology. I make no metaphysical assertions and even in my heart I am no Neo-Manichean; on the contrary I am deeply convinced of the unity of the self, as demonstrated by the mandala symbolism."(35)

Jung is afraid that if evil is looked upon as non-being, **"nobody will take his own shadow seriously...The future of mankind very much depends upon the recognition of the shadow.** Evil is - psychologically speaking - **terribly real.** It is a fatal mistake to diminish its power and reality even merely metaphysically. I am sorry, this goes to the very roots of Christianity."(36)

Jung's position from a psychological perspective is clear and understandable, and it is puzzling that Fr. White would misinterpret it as a quasi-Manichean dualism if he were viewing it simply from this point of view. But there is something more at stake here. When Jung says, "It is a fatal mistake to diminish its power and reality even merely metaphysically. I am sorry, this goes to the very roots of Christianity", we have a premonition of the thoughts that were to blossom in the **Answer to Job.** Does the phrase "merely metaphysically" suffer under the same defects as the expression Jung so disliked of "nothing but"? Does Jung mean that metaphysics must look to psychology for the way it describes evil, or metaphysics is merely a reflection of psychological truth, or finally, the dualism of good and evil goes to the roots of Christianity and psychology is faced with the unpleasant task of putting things back together again? Thus, if Jung is uneasy about the problem of evil from a psychological point of view, Fr. White is disquieted when he views the metaphysical implications of Jung's statements. The problem of the privatio boni rests on the foundation of the question of the relationship between Jung's psychology and metaphysics. Jung wanted to keep to his psychological point of view, and thus he says, "Your metaphysical thinking "posits" mine doubts, i.e., it weighs mere names for insufficiently known (substances)."(37) He goes on to say that he can only assimilate a "substance", but substance in this case has nothing to do with substance in the philosophical sense, but it is simply the ground and guarantee of phenomena. There must be something underlying the phenomena and giving it coherence. He accuses Fr. White of being able to deal with a concept like non-being because White is concerned only with conceptual existence and not with real things, and he concludes, "That is, I suppose, the reason why the unconscious turns for you into a system of abstract conceptions."(38) This same line of reasoning appears in a letter to Gebhard Frei in which Jung sees a "clash between scientific and epistemological thinking on the one hand and theological and metaphysical thinking on the other."(39) Jung feels that his "critics actually **believe only in words**, without knowing it, and then think they have **posited God**."(40) The theologians, in Jung's mind, mistake their concepts for real things, while Jung feels he rightly limits himself to the Imago Dei: "My thinking is **substantive**, but theological-metaphysical thinking is in constant danger...of operating with substanceless words and imagining that the reality corresponding to them is then seated in Heaven."(41)

Jung never viewed the privatio boni from a metaphysical point of view, and he had no wish to do so and no appreciation that there could be a legitimate metaphysical point of view, and while Fr. White sometimes criticized Jung's psychological conceptions in a philosophical light, and thus misconstrued them, he was also fighting to preserve the ground on which he stood. If there is no legitimate metaphysical or theological point of view, how could he maintain his Catholic faith?

Jung's discussion with White continued at great length, but without ever overcoming this misunderstanding. In June of 1952 Jung wrote about the problem of the privatio boni: "The crux seems to lie in the contamination of the two incongruous notions of Good and of Being. If you assume, as I do, that Good is a moral judgment and not substantial in itself, then Evil is its opposite and just as non-substantial as the first. If however you assume that Good is Being, then Evil can be nothing else than Non-

Being."(42) This is an excellent summary of the problem.
Jung finds that good and evil as moral judgments are obvious facts, but, "There is not the faintest evidence for
the identity of Good and Being."(43) Here the difficulty
is precisely the question of what kind of evidence. Psychological facts are not metaphysical facts, and evidence for
empirical psychology is not evidence for metaphysics.

Later that summer Victor White again stayed at Jung's
retreat at Bollingen, but apparently this discussion was
deadlocked. After this visit their correspondence began to
ebb away. Jung's few letters to Fr. White seem to come
as responses to Fr. White's own, which appear to deal with
his deepening conflict between his role in the Church and
his adherence to Jung's psychology. Jung answered these
letters at length, elaborating his notions on the nature of
the Godhead from his distinctive point of view. Far from
encouraging Fr. White to leave his position in the Church,
he developed arguments for the value of Fr. White's work
within the institutional setting. At the same time, unwittingly, he could have made Victor White's inner struggles
more difficult. Despite Jung's affirmations that he is not
interested in making metaphysical statements, the impact
of his statements about God, precisely because he does not
think that either metaphysics or theology is a viable way
of knowing, can create the impression in the Catholic
reader that this interpretation of the nature of God is
incompatible with Catholic faith. It stands as a radical
alternative to the traditional understanding because it at
once limits itself to the psychological point of view, while
at the same time negates the epistemological validity of
knowing through faith. There is a very good chance that
Fr. White was living out this difficulty. He was aware of
the power and value of Jung's psychology, and the need
the Catholic Church had of it, but try as he may, he
could not swallow the implicit philosophical implications.

Jung, in a letter to E.V. Tenney, in February 1955,
gives his view of Fr. White's problem:

"Another aspect of this concretism is the rigidity of
scholastic philosophy, through which Father White is wrig-
gling as well as he can. He is at bottom an honest and
sincere man who cannot but admit the importance of psychology, but the trouble is that he gets into an awful stew
about it. Analytical psychology unfortunately just touches
the vulnerable spot of the church, viz. the untenable con-

cretism of its beliefs, and the syllogistic character of Thomistic philosophy. This is of course a terrific snag, but - one could almost say - fortunately people are unaware of the clashing contrasts. Father White, however, is by no means unconscious of those clashes; it is a very serious personal problem to him."(44)

Is this "untenable concretism" no less the belief on the part of the Catholics that God, Jesus, Mary, etc., can be known in some measure in themselves through revelation?

This "awful stew" of Fr. White, which was an epistemological one, is probably what gave birth to his intemperate criticisms of Jung's **Answer to Job.** In contrast to his initial enthusiastic reception of the book, in his review of the English translation he asks whether: "Jung is pulling our leg or is duped by some Satanic trickster into purposefully torturing his friends and devotees."(45) "Or is he, more rationally, purposefully putting them to the test to discover how much they will stand rather than admit the fallibility of their master..."(46) This public outburst was more than enough to break their already fragile relationship.

For Jung it was a real disappointment and, no doubt, a blow to his feelings especially because of the affection he had lavished on Fr. White: "As there are so few men capable of understanding the deeper implications of our psychology, I had nursed the apparently vain hope that Fr. Victor would carry on the magnum opus."(47)

After 1955 they drifted apart, only to try to draw together again at the time of Fr. White's last illness. Old feelings of affection had endured during the intervening years, but there was still no new understanding from either side to break the impasse. Victor White died on the 22nd of May, 1960.

The effect of reading Jung's letters to Victor White is one of sympathy for both men. When we see Jung, for example, trying to write a letter to Fr. White from his sick bed after his almost fatal heart attack, we cannot help but feel the intensity of his desire to make contact with him, and through him, to wrestle with his own fate of trying to bring his inner experiences into relationship with Christian thought. Neither can we withhold our sympathy for Fr. White if we imagine him in the tower at Bollingen, listening to Jung's discussions about God that had all the power of immediate experience and the convic-

tion that comes from it. The deeper Victor White entered
into Jung's world, the more the tension grew between his
Catholic faith, strengthened and elaborated by his theological work, and Jung's religious views. His espousal of Jung's
psychology was costing him dearly in the ecclesiastical
world in which he lived, but it was creating even more
serious problems within.

In summary, the valuable discoveries that Jung made
are wrapped in accidental philosophical and religious attitudes. Jung's statements on the scope of our ability to
know should be interpreted only in relationship to his
natural science of the psyche and not extended to philosophy or theology. Once the distinction is made between the
essence of his work and the context it developed in, the
way is open to employ it as an instrument in Christian
theology. Two dangers can then be avoided, that is, to
treat his psychology as a substitute for theology or to
reject it outright as a danger to it.

PART II

THE DAWN OF CONTEMPLATION

CHAPTER 3

ST. JOHN AND THE BEGINNING OF CONTEMPLATION

An introduction to St. John's doctrine, even when we limit ourselves to his less daunting discussions of the beginning of the mystical life, suffers from some of the same limitations that are found in reading Jung's works; we are dealing with formulations that are meant to be lived out and practiced, and not simply understood intellectually. For St. John mystical experience, which he also called infused contemplation, meant a real experience of union with God, and his writings stressed the way in which a person must conduct himself in order to attain to this union and the sufferings that he must undergo.

JOHN OF THE CROSS

Juan de Yepes was born in Spain in the Castillian town of Fontiveros in 1542. Soon after his birth his father died, and his mother had to struggle to keep her three young sons alive. This poverty probably played a role in the death of one of John's brothers and the move of the family to Medina del Campo, where John was placed in an orphanage. Upon leaving the orphanage in his teens he served as a nurse in a hospital of incurables, and attended the Jesuit college.

At 21 he decided to enter the Carmelite monastery in

Medina del Campo. After being ordained as a priest he was at the point of leaving the Order for a more rigorous and secluded one when he met Teresa of Avila who had already initiated a reform movement for the sisters, and was planning one for the friars as well. She convinced him to help her in this new work, and he started the first house of the new reform and went on to hold many positions in this growing movement.

In 1577, while in the midst of an extended stay as a confessor and spiritual director at St. Teresa's convent at Avila, he was kidnapped by the friars who opposed the reform and was imprisoned at Toledo. Buried in a dark cell and treated brutally, he began to fear for his life. Here he suffered a dark night out of which was born some of his most beautiful poetry. After more than eight months of torment he escaped and went south to Andalusia. Charged with the spiritual direction of St. Teresa's sisters, he began to teach and write maxims as aids to their devotion, and eventually undertake his prose works which were intended to be commentaries on his major poems. After many years, dividing his time in administering the growing reform and dedicating himself to the task of spiritual direction, he again fell afoul of some of his fellow friars. He was harassed and removed from all office, fell ill and died in 1591 at 49 years of age. The manuscripts of his writings circulated widely both inside and outside his order until they were printed in 1618.

WRITINGS ON THE PASSAGE TO CONTEMPLATION

Three of St. John's four major works concern us directly because they each contain a long passage devoted to the beginning of contemplation: the **Ascent of Mount Carmel**, its companion piece the **Dark Night of the Soul**, and the **Living Flame of Love**. The latter deals with the highest reaches of mysticism, and its treatment of the passage to contemplation is incidental to the main theme of the work. In the **Ascent** and **Dark Night**, however, this doctrine is found in the context of the development of the whole life of prayer.

READING ST. JOHN

The first reading of the **Ascent** or **Dark Night** can be disconcerting, for it is hard to find the proper perspective in which to view them. These two books, though conceived as parts of one over-all plan, form only a loose unity. The **Ascent of Mount Carmel** started as a commentary on the poem, "On a Dark Night", and was, as well, an exposition of a diagram that St. John had drawn illustrating how to ascend the mount of perfection which he used as an aid in spiritual direction. These original purposes were gradually submerged under the force of the logical flow of his explanations. Only the first stanzas of the poem were ever commented on, the diagram of the mount receded into the background, and the entire treatise of the **Ascent** was never finished. The book the **Dark Night** tends to complete the original undertaking, but it has the marks of being written separately with its own terminology and point of view. The **Ascent-Dark Night** is a disconcerting mixture of poetry and prose, psychological descriptions and scholastic doctrine that is saved from confusion by the unrelenting intent of the author which turns it into a masterpiece of the interior life. This intent is to actually guide the reader to the goal of union with God.

St. John was not primarily a writer, and he did not set out to create systematic treatises of mystical theology. In the prologue to the **Ascent of Mount Carmel**, after ennumerating some of the problems that demand attention, he explains:

"Our goal will be, with God's help, to explain all these points, so that everyone who reads this book will in some way discover the road that he is walking along, and the one he ought to follow if he wants to reach the summit of this mount."(1)

The accent is on this practical work of how to actually climb the mountain, and St. John had little time for people who proposed to travel to God in pleasant and delectable ways. Since there was nothing that could compare with this goal, everything else must be left behind. St. John's writings have often been called negative and privative because of this thoroughgoing detachment. Yet when he wrote, he had already climbed high on the mountain and was trying to guide his penitents to the same height and did not want them to dawdle on the road distracted by non-essential things. The apparent complexity and the detailed landscape of the **Ascent** and the **Dark Night** resolves itself into a single-pointed vision once we take up St. John's perspective. The end is divine union, and all else must be laid aside. This union cannot be achieved by means of sense knowledge, nor even by spiritual ideas and feelings about God. The **Ascent** and **Dark Night** devote themselves to subtly and exhaustively analyzing how our attachment to worldly things and even spiritual goods can hinder the attainment of the highest good. In fact, it is the attachment to spiritual blessings in the form of the consolation of prayer, visions and revelations that pose the most dangerous obstacles because they are felt to be good and are clung to.

St. John, although he asks for a complete and penetrating detachment from all that is not God Himself, does not consider it a work of human effort alone. What is given up is replaced by something better. The giving up of temporal and worldly desires takes place under the advent of spiritual desires and experiences which more than make up for them, and later, the giving up of these spiritual desires is the prelude to the beginning of contemplation and is caused by the advent of this new experience.

This spiritual program leading to divine union is based on a number of premises which St. John derived from the scholastic philosophy he was trained in and applied to the life of prayer:

"The cause of this darkness is attributable to the fact that - as the scholastic philosophers say - the soul is like a **tabula rasa** (a clean slate) when God infuses it into the body, so that it would be ignorant without the knowledge it receives through its senses, because no knowledge is communicated to it from any other source. Accordingly, the presence of the soul in the body resembles the presence of a prisoner in a dark dungeon, who knows no more than what he manages to behold through the windows of his prison and has nowhere else to turn if he sees nothing through them. For the soul, naturally speaking, possesses no means other than the senses (the windows of its prison) of perceiving what is communicated to it."(2)

The conclusion to this line of reasoning is that if a man denies what comes through his senses, his soul would be in darkness and empty, and though a man must sense, if he desires not to do so, he attains the same effect as if he did not sense at all.

The reason why the mortification of desire is so important is that a disordered desire creates a likeness between the person and what he desires, "For love effects a likeness between the lover and the object loved."(3) If a person has inordinate desires for things other than God, he or she becomes made over in their likeness and cannot be made in the likeness of God. This dual affection cannot exist because two contraries cannot coexist in one person; darkness which is affection set upon creatures and light which is God are contrary to each other.

St. John's conclusion is that if a man becomes like the limited object of his desire, he cannot realize his potential to be transformed into the likeness of the infinite God, for such transformation demands that the will of man be completely in accord with the will of God, and any voluntary imperfection is enough to create an obstacle to this transformation. This doctrine forms the general context to the beginning of contemplation and the rationale underlying the "dark night (the mortification of the appetites and the denial of pleasure in all things) for the attainment of the divine union with God."(4)

MEDITATION

St. John starts his description of the life of prayer with conversion and the state of beginners:

"It should be known, then, that God nurtures and caresses the soul, after it has been resolutely converted to His service, like a loving mother who warms her child with the heat of her bosom, nurses it with good milk and tender food, and carries and caresses it in her arms."(5)

Before this time the beginner had been attached to the things of the world, but now a dramatic change has taken place, for the soul which had been circumscribed by the world now becomes inflamed with love for spiritual things and the love for the world is replaced by the love for the things of God. Here there is no purely negative asceticism. Undoubtedly, the beginner must make strong efforts to break with his former habits, but these efforts are powerfully aided by the new yearnings of love that have sprung up within. The transition from the world to the beginning of the spiritual life is explained by St. John in the **Ascent** when he comments on the words "an enkindling with longings of love":

"The love of one's Spouse is not the only requisite for

conquering the strength of the sensitive appetites; an enkindling with longings of love is also necessary. For the
sensory appetites are moved and attracted toward sensory
objects with such cravings that if the spiritual part of the
soul is not fired with other more urgent longings for spiritual things, the soul will neither be able to overcome the
yoke of nature nor enter the night of sense; nor will it
have the courage to live in the darkness of all things by
denying its appetites for them."(6)

The prayer of these beginners is what St. John calls
meditation. Meditation today, when it is applied to spiritual practices, usually gives the impression of being a very
orderly and rational analysis of a spiritual topic which
gives rise to affective resolutions by way of conclusions
to the reasoning process. For St. John, however, meditation
is more generic and covers a great deal more ground.

Meditation as described in the **Ascent** centers around
the faculty of imagination. But the imagination is not
conceived of in isolation. It draws its raw material from
the senses and then elaborates and develops these images
through the use of the intellect, memory and will. Meditation embraces all the kinds of prayer that a person can
make by his own efforts.

If meditation is the spiritual activity of the beginner,
then the "longings of love" represent how the soul is acted
upon. The two go together to form a harmonious unity
which is best described as sensible spirituality or sensible
religious experience. Before conversion the beginner was
bound to the world, and his attention, affection, energy
and faculties were devoted to worldly things by means of
the senses; the beginner looked outward through the senses
toward the world.

Conversion alters this picture 180°, and now the new
spiritual yearnings take the place of the attraction of the
world. The beginner turns his attention, energy and faculties to spiritual things but, and here is the crucial point,
he does it again by means of the senses, that is, by the
natural faculties that work through the senses. The new
attraction that arises in the spiritual part of the soul
begins to counterbalance the sensible attraction for the
world and soon overpowers it. The focus of attention and
desire begins to rotate like a compass needle under a
greater magnetic force. Attention and energy turn inward
but it is attention, energy and natural operation of the

faculties that only know how to operate through the senses. Therefore, the net effect of initial conversion is that the desire for temporal things becomes a sensible appreciation of spiritual things, the two being, in fact, opposite perspectives from the same vantage point.

Another way of explaining this process is by saying that grace must initially take man as he is. The phase of sensible spirituality is a necessary stage, and in St. John's mind it serves as a remote preparation for divine union:

"For though the apprehensions of these faculties are not a proximate means toward union for proficients, they are a remote means for beginners. By these sensitive means beginners dispose their spirit and habituate it to spiritual things, and at the same time they void their senses of all other base, temporal, secular, and natural forms and images."(7)

But sensible spirituality is only a remote preparation, for it labors under inherent difficulties. Its most fundamental limitation springs from the fact that the senses can never adequately contain the spiritual, and therefore will always give a fragmentary and inadequate account of it. Furthermore, in regards to purity of intention, the soul is drawn to spiritual things not so much by what they are in themselves, for its understanding of their true nature is very limited, but more by the pleasure and consolation it finds in them. Sensible pleasure, then, is often a prime driving force. It is from this source of motivation that arises part of the fervor of beginners with their ability to spend hours in prayer and to devote themselves to penance and discipline, for all these things, as strange as it may seem, are sweet and enjoyable to them. St. John describes the faults and weaknesses of these beginners at great length in the first part of his **Dark Night of the Soul**. This sensible spirituality forms the point of departure from which the transition to contemplation begins.

CONTEMPLATION

Faith and divine union are the two key concepts that allow us to understand what St. John means by contemplation. In the **Ascent**, in order to illustrate the meaning of union, St. John uses the image of a pane of glass in the rays of the sun; the more the glass is purified the more it is transformed by the sunlight. It retains its own nature but becomes the sun by participation:

"And God will so communicate His supernatural being to it that it will appear to be God Himself and will possess all that God Himself has."(8)

This conception of divine union is far from any pantheism, for man's nature remains distinct, but it is also far removed from any simply moral union in which a man might be called God-like because he obeys the law of God. Divine union in St. John's mind is a real participation in God's life through knowledge and love. If divine union is the goal, faith is the means. But St. John's conception of faith is not easy to grasp even for the person pursuing the life of prayer. "Like a blind man he must lean on dark faith, accept it for his guide and light, and rest on nothing of what he understands, tastes, feels, or imagines."(9)

The reality of faith so transcends human nature that St. John disconcertingly likens trying to explain it to attempting to describe colors to a blind man. Faith:

"deprives and blinds a person of any other knowledge or science by which he may judge it. Other knowledge is acquired by the light of the intellect, but not the knowledge that faith gives. Faith nullifies the light of the intellect, and if this light is not darkened, the knowledge of faith is lost."(10)

Faith is seen as a supernatural way of knowing quite diverse in object and inner dynamism from all natural knowing. No knowledge coming to man through his senses or rational faculties can bring him in contact with God in order that he can know Him as He is. Only faith is the proximate and proportionate means of knowing God in this way. Its proximity is rooted in its divine origin in the gift of grace which transforms man and elevates his natural powers. Man must cling to faith even though this seems to quench his natural modes of knowing.

And it is the clinging of the old man to his limited way of perceiving and experiencing that hinder this necessary reliance on faith. It is especially the clinging to spiritual knowledge, which is good in itself, that creates an obstacle to divine union; the limited lights of spiritual knowledge coming through the natural faculties appear brighter to the soul than the light of faith. In reality the light of faith is much greater, but manifests itself in another way, so it initially appears as darkness to the soul.

Several words of clarification on this doctrine of St. John are in order. First of all, faith as a proximate means of union with God was always understood by him to be working in and through love and never apart from it.

Secondly, union with God, though it is beyond the natural capacity of man, is still a real experience, in fact, the most real experience according to St. John. Divine union, however, transcends man's natural power not only by the sublimity of its object but by the way it attains it. Ordinarily the intellect functions in a discriminatory way; it breaks down the reality to be known into small insights or concepts, and then unite these concepts to form a more or less adequate judgment about the reality. The discursive intellect sees things piecemeal, as it were, not as wholes, not as possessing a within. We know about things and about people; we do not know people directly in their subjectivity, which is a great limitation, for it is there that they are most themselves. Still less do we know God from within, only at a distance in the prism of creatures.

St. John implies that the experience of contemplation is an intersubjective experience. The person experiences God within him, not as an object or thing about which something is known, but simply as a whole, a subject. God is present to him in a way analogous to the way he is present to himself.

"At this time God does not communicate Himself through the senses as He did before, by means of the discursive analysis and synthesis of ideas, but begins to communicate Himself through pure spirit by an act of simple contemplation, in which there is no discursive succession of thought."(11)

It is love in informing and vivifying faith that allows faith to attain to this sort of knowledge. Love of its nature is geared to the subject, and divine love lifts the person to a subject-to-subject relationship to God. Contemplation "which is knowledge and love together, that is, loving knowledge"(12) is the beginning of the experience of this new relationship. In it love is strong enough that it draws knowledge with it, so there results an experience of the within, God present as a self in the heart of the limited human self.

In sharp contrast to ordinary prayer where God is thought and felt about, the chief note of contemplation

is that God's presence is experienced; this presence is initially felt within as some sort of interior touch. This
experiential knowledge of God brings with itself other
characteristics. It is felt to be independent of the will of
the person receiving it, varying in intensity, demanding
less effort than meditation and impeding in some fashion
the natural workings of the soul. This knowledge of God
remains obscure, and the mode of its communication not
comprehended.

FROM MEDITATION TO CONTEMPLATION

As long as consolation and sweetness remain, the beginner is satisfied that God is approving of his life of prayer.
However, for those called to contemplation this state cannot last. It is here, after the soul has become accustomed
to the feelings and consolations of beginners, that St. John
introduces the night of sense. Consolation and sweetness
begin to diminish and aridity seizes the soul. The sense
of value and accomplishment in praying evaporates. The
night of sense is the beginning of contemplation; St. John
calls it arid, purgative contemplation or dark fire. It is
the herald of the more perceptible contemplation to come,
and its purpose is to detach the soul from sensible knowledge and prepare it for this higher way of knowing.

The beginning of contemplation is often gradual and
blends imperceptibly with the simplification of ordinary
prayer. However, it can also take place in a sudden and
disconcerting fashion. This latter case is instructive because it points to the underlying discontinuity of the two
states. St. John has likened this transitional stage to the
weaning from the breast of sensible consolations, and to
the shutting out of the sun of divine favor.

"Consequently, it is at the time they are going about
their spiritual exercises with delight and satisfaction, when
in their opinion the sun of divine favor is shining most
brightly on them, that God darkens all this light and
closes the door and spring of the sweet spiritual water
they were tasting as often and as long as they desired."
(13)

The heights of consolation for the beginner often have
a mystical flavor to them; there is a certain savour and
experience and sense of the presence of God which is best
described as the sensible analogate of contemplative exper-

ience. Unfortunately, the limitations of this state are quite hidden from the person experiencing these consolations. For this reason the sudden cessation of consolation is experienced as a terrible trial. There is intense soul-searching for the reason why it has happened. There is a fruitless search for the unrepented sin which must underlie God's apparent anger. The resultant anxiety is more oppressive than the loss of consolation itself, for it centers on the apparent loss of God. The frantic attempts to recapture this lost sense of communion by a return to meditation and spiritual practices is doomed to failure, and only exacerbate the predominant mood of anxiety. Seen objectively, it is clear that the person is already learning the necessary distinction between sensible consolation and God Himself by means of this privation, but subjectively he is convinced that God has left him.

The onset of this process of weaning according to St. John, whether it is gradual or sudden, does not necessarily take a long time. He says that with people who wholeheartedly take up the spiritual life it can happen rather quickly. They have obtained the habit of meditation and derived substantially what they should have from its practice. The destination of the journey has been reached and the fruit has been peeled and is ready to be eaten. Meditation has served to accomodate sense to spirit, and now a mysterious new experience is beginning.

Unfortunately, the person undergoing this experience without any guidance tends to feel that it is, indeed, negative and privative rather than positive. He strives to go back to his former ways of praying with the result that he hinders this new experience from taking hold.

Even sadder than the misunderstanding of the beginner is the virtual absence of adequate direction. This grave lack of direction is what prompted St. John to return again and again to a detailed description of this predicament and the practical remedy for it. It also forced from him some of the most vehement denouncements to be found in all his writings. He likens the erring directors to blacksmiths who know only how to pound on the delicate workings of the soul, and to crude artisans who clumsily dab away at beautiful paintings, smearing them with strange colors, instead of leading them gently into the necessary detachment and simplicity.

The soul's lack of understanding and poor direction are

compounded in St. John's mind by the work of the devil. The evil one takes his stand with great cunning on the road which leads from sense to spirit. He tries with all his wiles to prevent the soul from passing over into this higher state of prayer where he can meddle with much less effectiveness. He torments them, especially those called to greater perfection, with severe temptations in the form of scrupulosity, urges to blaspheme and sins against chastity.

Therefore, though many enter this night of sense which heralds the beginning of contemplation, few successfully emerge. Since contemplation is an essentially new experience, it is difficult to get used to. St. John, therefore, sets down three signs by which the beginner can make a judgment of whether he is really being led into the contemplative state.

The first sign is that he cannot meditate any longer or find that sweetness which used to come through the exercise of his faculties. The second sign is that he does not have a desire to fix his attention and thoughts on other things besides the spiritual.

"The third and surest sign is that a person likes to remain alone in loving awareness of God, without particular considerations, in interior peace and quiet and repose, and without the acts and exercises (at least discursive, those in which one progresses from point to point) of the intellect, memory and will; and that he prefers to remain only in the general, loving awareness and knowledge we mentioned, without any particular knowledge or understanding."(14)

Since the first sign might result from lukewarmness, neglect or sin, the second sign is used as a safeguard, and since the first and second signs might be the result of some illness or general weakness where the soul has no desire for anything, the third sign is brought forth. The third is the most vital sign, for it is that of contemplation itself. Since the recipient is still addicted to sense perception, this new knowledge is too different and subtle to be readily perceptible. However, it will soon become so:

"But the more habituated he becomes to this calm, the deeper his experience of the general, loving knowledge of God will grow. This knowledge is more enjoyable than all other things, because without the soul's labor it affords peace, rest, savor, and delight."(15)

The actual beginning of this infused contemplation is the crucial sign, for without it the soul would be leaving meditation without something better taking its place:

"If a man did not have this knowledge or attentiveness to God, he would, as a consequence, be neither doing anything nor receiving anything. Having left the discursive meditation of the sensitive faculties and still lacking contemplation (the general knowledge in which the spiritual faculties - memory, intellect, and will - are actuated and united in this passive, prepared knowledge), he would have no activity whatsoever relative to God."(16)

Contemplation does not come through the senses and thus to the rational faculties following the usual pattern of knowing, but rather it comes from behind, so to speak. It is infused directly into the rational faculties at their root, or center, so that the person receiving this knowledge does not understand how it got there except that it is the work of God and the presence of God. The basic human orientation of the rational faculties to knowledge which is sense-related plays havoc with the reception of contemplative knowledge; the whole tonality of the intellect looks towards the senses, and effectively blinds it to knowledge coming in any other way. It is literally looking in the wrong direction and does not know that there is another direction, and if it did know of this other direction, it would look at it with its conceptualizing and discriminating eyes and thus not see anything.

"So delicate is this refreshment that ordinarily, if a man have desire or care to experience it, he experiences it not; for, as I say, it does its work when the soul is most at ease and freest from care; it is like the air which, if one would close one's hand upon it, escapes."(17)

In order to perceive this new reality, the soul must abandon all its discursive activity and become like that which it is to receive.

"Since God, then, as the giver communes with him through a simple, loving knowledge, the individual also, as the receiver, communes with God, through a simple and loving knowledge or attention, so that knowledge is thus joined with knowledge and love with love. The receiver should act according to the mode of what is received, and not otherwise, in order to receive and keep it in the way it is given."(18)

The beginner must overcome his feelings of anxiety

he is doing nothing because he is not working with the natural faculties. His work, rather, is receiving.

"They must be content simply with a loving and peaceful attentiveness to God, and live without the concern, without the effort, and without the desire to taste or feel Him. All these desires disquiet the soul and distract it from the peaceful quiet and sweet idleness of the contemplation which is being communicated to it."(19)

St. John's teaching can be summarized as follows: the beginner experiences a growing difficulty in meditation through no conscious neglect or unknown illness. This decrease in the ability to meditate goes hand-in-hand with a desire to remain still and at peace, resting in a new contemplative knowledge of God that is being given to it. Though this knowledge is very faint and sometimes imperceptible at the beginning, it soon grows more and more conscious when the person learns what attitude to take up in regard to it; he then recognizes the presence of God within.

The dark night of sense, instead of being an abandonment by God, is in reality the beginning of a deeper communion with Him. The darkness is not the result of privation but unaccustomed brightness, and if the soul submits to it and takes up the proper attitude, it will soon perceive that this is so.

CHAPTER 4

A REVOLUTION OF MYSTICAL CONSCIOUSNESS

I have presented St. John's beginning of contemplation as a straightforward transition from meditation to infused contemplation. But before we go on to examine the interplay between individuation and contemplation in his life and doctrine, we have to make an important detour.

Soon after St. John wrote, another interpretation of his teaching on this time of transition developed. It went by the name of acquired or active contemplation and gave many of the passages cited in the last chapter a very different meaning. In essence, the promoters of acquired contemplation saw another alternative to the transition from meditation to infused contemplation. They felt meditation could lead to a contemplation based on our own efforts in the form of a simple, loving gaze at God, and they interpreted St. John's writings in this way. Both interpretations have co-existed and intermingled down to our own time, and if we do not sort them out we might well end up trying to renew the life of prayer not on the basis of St. John's authentic thoughts but, unwittingly, on a subsequent interpretation of him. In order to discriminate between the two I will examine St. John's teaching in more detail in this chapter and attempt to untangle some of the history of acquired contemplation in the next.

When St. Teresa and St. John wrote, they drew on the age-old mystical traditions of Western Christianity.(1) At the same time they transcended their sources and inaugurated a revolution of mystical consciousness. It was one of those privileged moments in the history of thought where things that had been formerly joined and intermixed in a lived unity, and thus lived out but not differentiated, now became articulated in their own right. When St. John carefully distinguished contemplation from ordinary prayer

and all accidental phenomena, whether natural or supernatural, he posed the issue of contemplation with a sharp-
ness and decisiveness it never had before. Those who came
after him could ask, were even compelled to ask, "Am I
a contemplative?" "Do I find in myself the three signs
that St. John gives?" Since the two great Carmelite saints
depicted contemplation as the full flowering of the interior
life, the spiritual writers who came after them tried to
reconcile this perspective with their own inner experiences. They had to say to themselves, "Since I am devoting
myself to the interior life, in what way am I a contemplative?"

The 17th century became a veritable spiritual labora-
tory in which men and women tried to assimilate this new
awareness of the centrality of contemplation in the life
of prayer. People then, just like people today, faced the
dilemma of the dark night of sense in the wider meaning
of the term. They had embraced the life of prayer, seriously devoted themselves to spiritual exercises, experienced
satisfaction and consolation in this new way of life and,
in short, fulfilled St. John's description of fervent beginners. Then, either gradually or suddenly, they lost this
sense of well-being and inner spiritual progress. They found
within themselves St. John's first two signs. They could
not meditate like they did before, nor did they have a new
interest in worldly things. Were they not, they asked
themselves, in the dark night that St. John described, and
therefore on their way to contemplation?

Unfortunately, the dark night seemed to go on and on
without ending in the perception of this new experience
of contemplation, and in the light of this experience of
darkness they began to reread St. John's writings. Since
they found within themselves these two signs, they were
encouraged by this confirmation to unwittingly reinterpret
his third and most vital sign, which was the presence of
contemplation itself. The relatively brief time of transition
that St. John had envisioned became extended to cover
months, or even years, and to form a distinct state or
stage of the spiritual life. The loving attentiveness that
in St. John's mind was an amalgamation of infused contemplation itself and the attitude of receptivity on the
part of the contemplative in the face of the actual experience became reduced to an active exercise of faith by
which someone believed God to be present and tried to

be attentive to this presence by faith, not by experience. St. John's challenge to contemplation and the heights of the mystical life was reduced to a much more lowly human scale. His view of the spiritual life which found infused contemplation as the natural flowering of the life of prayer was met by attempts to change his doctrine into one of active or acquired contemplation. These changes do not appear to have been deliberate. The men who created the various schools of acquired contemplation sincerely believed they were faithfully following in St. John's footsteps. For St. John the ideal solution to the problem of the dark night was the beginning of infused contemplation, but for these men of the 17th century who never arrived at this gift, their own predicament dictated new answers, and these new answers resonated with the times and echoed down the generations and effect the way we view contemplation today. Thus, the answer to the challenge of contemplation of the 17th century is important not only because it is still being lived out today, but it had a profound influence on the way contemplation is understood and viewed as a viable activity.

MYSTICISM IN THE TIME OF ST. JOHN

Soon after a strong current of interest in things mystical appeared in Spain at the beginning of the 16th century and found certain affinities with the humanism of Erasmus and the reform of Luther, it came to the attention of the Spanish Inquisition. This mystical current made up of many parts both sober and fantastic, orthodox and dubious, was counter-balanced by a growing thoroughness of the inquisitorial process. Along with a genuine awakening and development of the contemplative spirit there existed a whole spectrum of exaggeration and parody. Wandering holy women abounded with trances and swoons, and miraculous happenings were discerned in the most trivial events. It was a time of excess and credulity. One strand of this complex tapestry was given the label Illuminism. In theory, the Illuminists believed in the primacy of interior prayer carried to the extreme of the suppression of mental acts and the fulfillment of all obligations by this prayer to the detriment of vocal prayer and other external acts of worship. They are said to have believed in personal inspiration which freed the inspired from outward observances and led

to a belief in impeccability and consequent immoral behavior. In practice, it is difficult to tell who the Illuminists actually were and what they held. The inquisitorial
practices of unnamed accusors and confessions produced
by torture make the evidence and the convictions based
upon it suspect.

With the revolt of Luther the organized church of Spain
felt the need to impose its authority and crush any hint
that seemed to suggest its external practices were in need
of reform. This authoritarian temper distrusted mysticism
in general and began to look upon these people as if they
were at least potential heretics, if not actual ones. The
rigidity of the Inquisition militated against its possession
of a sensitivity by which it could distinguish the true from
the false mystics. Its brutal methods created an atmosphere of poisonous mistrust that surrounded the aspirations
of those seeking inner experience.

The Inquisition hovered in the background around such
notable figures as John of Avila, Luis of Granada, and
Ignatius Loyola. St. Teresa and St. John themselves had
their writings scrutinized by it, and there is the strong
possibility that this climate of suspicion prevented many
perfectly orthodox spiritual writers from expressing themselves clearly about the mystical path. St. John, therefore,
had to resist two very different kinds of pressures: the
first came from a popular taste for visions, revelations and
extravagant penances, and at times his confreres could not
understand his lack of interest in such things. The second
came from the Inquisition and the inquisitorial mentality
that grew up in his own order with the ascendancy of
Nicholas Doria as Provincial. John, who upheld the primacy
of contemplation, the independence of the Carmelite sisters from central control, who had a distaste for perma-
nent office-holding, and who wrote extensively on the
passivity of the faculties in contemplation, must have
appeared all too close to dangerous ground to this type
of authoritarian mind.

It is not surprising, then, that there was not any rush
to publish St. John's writings in the years immediately
following his death in 1591. It was not until 1601 that the
matter was brought up, and it was not successfully concluded until 1618.

FROM MEDITATION TO CONTEMPLATION

The heart of the question of acquired or active contemplation is whether St. John actually taught such a doctrine. Ironically, it is partially because of the great care he took in describing the transition to contemplative prayer and the subtle descriptions he gave of it precisely because he did not want it misunderstood, that have occasioned its misunderstanding. The very intricate structure of this doctrine and its psychological acuity make it liable to be misinterpreted in a lesser and more human manner.

There are a number of points that govern the interpretation of St. John's writings on this crucial time of transformation, which can be summed up under the following headings: meditation, contemplation, activity and passivity, perceptibility, difficult texts and loving attentiveness.

What does he mean by meditation? Does he limit it to the use of the imagination and thus distinguish it from other kinds of working of the faculties? For example, is there a purely intellectual kind of intuition so that someone could stop meditating and still be doing something?

What is contemplation? Can we find in St. John any grounds for distinguishing two kinds of contemplation?

Meditation and contemplation are the beginning and the end of the process that St. John is describing, but what of the activity of the person during these changes? Can they be said to be active, or are they passively receiving this new experience?

Perceptibility. Is contemplation a real experience that is actually perceived, or can it remain hidden?

There are several problem texts which seem to point to the existence of an active contemplation and have been construed often in that sense.

Loving attentiveness. Is loving attentiveness a particular act by which a person takes up an attitude of attention to God Whom he believes present, or is it part and parcel of infused contemplation itself?

What is at stake here is not some fine points of scholastic theology but two very different conceptions of St. John which have many important practical ramifications for living out the interior life.

MEDITATION

St. John was aware, as a well-trained scholastic philosopher, of the distinctions between the natural faculties
of the soul, and he makes use of these distinctions between sense, imagination, intellect and will in the **Ascent
of Mount Carmel** when he analyzes their limitations as
proximate means of union with God. But in the practical
order, when it is a question of attaining to union with God
through contemplation, he groups all these faculties together under the heading of the natural working of the
faculties and he equates this natural working with meditation. He clearly points out that meditation is directly
dependent on the imagination and is "a discursive action
wrought by means of images, forms and figures that are
fashioned and imagined."(2) But imagination in its turn is
dependent on the sense, for "the imagination cannot fashion or imagine anything whatsoever beyond that which it
has experienced through its exterior senses."(3) But the
imagination is also linked with the process of reasoning.
St. John strings together "meditations, forms, and ideas",
(4) and talks of "the path of meditation and reasoning".(5)
He contrasts the knowledge of the soul in contemplation
with the knowledge that comes through "certain intelligible
forms which understanding or sense may seize upon"(6),
making it clear that the soul has left the use of "particular kinds of knowledge and intelligence"(7) which is the
food of the understanding and not simply just leaving
images. It is "detached and removed from all intelligible
forms which are objects of the understanding"(8). In speaking of contemplation he says, "For God now begins to
communicate Himself to it, no longer through sense, as
He did aforetime, by means of reflections which joined and
sundered its knowledge, but by pure spirit, into which
consecutive reflections enter not"(9).

CONTEMPLATION

If meditation is the active working of the faculties,
contemplation for St. John, which he describes under a
variety of terms, means infused contemplation which is
received without the natural use of the faculties. Some
of the many terms that St. John uses are: "one act that
is general and pure"(10); "this peace and rest of interior

quiet"(11); "loving general knowledge of God"(12); "substantial and loving quiet"(13); "confused and general knowledge"(14); "general and loving attentiveness or knowledge of God"(15); "general and supernatural knowledge and light"(16); "pure and serene light"(17); "pure and simple general light"(18); "quietness and ease"(19); "contemplation is naught else than a secret peaceful and loving infusion from God"(20); "this food is the infused contemplation whereof we have spoken"(21); "the way of illumination or of infused contemplation"(22); "contemplation, which is Divine love and knowledge in one - that is, a loving knowledge"(23); "infused with the spirit of Divine wisdom"(24); "this knowledge is general and dark"(25).

ACTIVITY AND PASSIVITY

Often these phrases describing contemplation are directly linked to the cessation of the active working of the faculties. "For, the farther the soul progresses in spirituality, the more it ceases from the operation of the faculties in particular acts, since it becomes more and more occupied in one act that is general and pure...the faculties... cease to work."(26) "...their soul, which was taking pleasure in being in that quietness and ease, instead of working with its faculties."(27) "...the way of illumination or of infused contemplation, wherein God Himself feeds and refreshes the soul, without meditation, or the soul's active help."(28) "For God secretly and quietly infuses into the soul loving knowledge and wisdom without any intervention of specific acts".(29) "Divine love and knowledge in one - that is, a loving knowledge, wherein the soul has not to use its natural acts and meditations."(30) "...no necessity for distinct knowledge nor for the soul to perform any acts, for God, in one act, is communicating to the soul loving knowledge."(31)

It follows if this contemplation does not depend on the natural work of the faculties and is an infused gift of God, then these faculties are passive in regard to it. "...the faculties are at rest, and are working, not actively, but passively, by receiving that which God works in them."(32) This passage goes on to say, "and, if they work at times, it is not with violence or with carefully elaborated meditation, but with sweetness of love, moved less by the ability of the soul itself than by God."(33)

PERCEPTIBILITY

The question of perceptible experience is at the heart of the problem of acquired contemplation. The later proponents of this doctrine would agree that St. John was talking about infused contemplation, but they would assert that this contemplation remained hidden, even for months or years. St. John does say, "It is true, however, that, when this condition first begins, the soul is hardly aware of this loving knowledge".(34) And this is because it is turned towards meditation and sense, and particular perceptions, and therefore not disposed to this new kind of experience. Thus, John calls the new experience imperceptible in relationship to the soul which is bound up in sense perceptions, but it is not imperceptible in itself, so he concludes the passage by saying, "But the more accustomed the soul grows to this, by allowing itself to rest, the more it will grow therein and the more conscious it will become of that loving general knowledge of God, in which it has greater enjoyment than in ought else, since this knowledge causes it peace, rest, pleasure and delight without labor." (35)

And when St. John says, "When the spiritual person cannot meditate, let him learn to be still in God, fixing his loving attention upon Him in the calm of his understanding, although he may think himself to be doing nothing" (36), it is foreign to his mind to be thinking that this loving attention is some kind of activity of the soul by which it gazes at God, even though it has no experience of Him, but simply is believing Him present. St. John in the next sentence states, "For thus, little by little and very quickly, Divine calm and peace will be infused into his soul, together with a wondrous and sublime knowledge of God, unfolded in Divine love."(37) This is a beautiful definition of infused contemplation, but it also clearly shows the experimental character of the knowledge that St. John expects to quickly become apparent once the soul ceases working with the faculties.

In the **Dark Night** when St. John is describing the second sign which is "that the memory is ordinarily centered upon God, with painful care and solicitude than before, in its anxiety not to fail God; and if it is not immediately conscious of spiritual sweetness and delight", this is because it is still too used to the operations of sense.(39) The soul is deriving strength and energy from the beginning of contemplation, and if this contemplation "is secret and hidden from the very person that experiences it"(40), yet far from this being a habitual state in which they will remain, St. John states in the very same number, "If those souls to whom this comes to pass knew how to be quiet at this time, and troubled not about performing any kind of action, whether inward or outward, neither had any anxiety about doing anything, then they would delicately experience this inward refreshment in that ease and freedom from care."(41) Thus, he again links up the hidden nature of the contemplation with its actual experience. It is hidden not because it should remain imperceptible, but because the soul is at the precise moment of transition where it is receiving the contemplative experience without realizing it must cease its discursive activities.

Finally, it is in the same way that we should understand John's subtle analysis of the very pure soul who receives a lofty and pure contemplation, and thus an experience that seems obscure and imperceptible in relationship to the working of the natural faculties.(42) It falls into a kind of forgetfulness, even for hours at a time, "and, when the soul returns to itself, it believes that less than a moment has passed, or no time at all."(43) Here St. John is working on a much more lofty plane than the common experience of someone who cannot meditate and yet hopes that something somehow is happening. Even in the kind of imperceptibility he is describing, there is some kind of powerful absorption taking place. And this forgetfulness happens only very seldom. "Only when God suspends in the soul the exercise of all its faculties."(44) Then even for this special case St. John concludes, "For, when it (the contemplative knowledge) is communicated to the will also, which happens almost invariably, the soul does not cease to understand in the very least degree, if it will reflect hereon, that it is employed and occupied in this knowledge, inasmuch as it is conscious of a sweetness of love therein, without particular knowledge or understanding of that which it loves."(45)

THREE DIFFICULT TEXTS

There are three passages that at first glance seem to

imply that St. John recognized an acquired contemplation. The first in the **Dark Night** deals with the way people are to conduct themselves in the dark night of sense and remain peaceful, even though it seems to them they are doing nothing:

"What they must do is merely to leave the soul free and disencumbered and at rest from all knowledge and thought, troubling not themselves, in that state, about what they shall think or meditate upon, but contenting themselves with merely a peaceful and loving attentiveness toward God, and in being without anxiety, without the ability and without desire to have experience of Him or to perceive Him."(46)

Isn't this an excellent summary of a state of prayer in which there is no experience, and the person praying takes up an attitude of loving attentiveness towards God? First of all, the phrase "to have experience of Him or to perceive Him" translates the original "sin gana de gustarle o de sentirle", which is literally "without the desire to taste or feel Him", which is how the Kavanaugh and Rodriguez translation puts it. What is at stake is not having no desire for any sort of perception or experience, but rather, St. John's often repeated advice that the particular kind of knowledge coming through the faculties hinder the reception of infused contemplation, and it is a question of the actual reception of contemplation, for St. John concludes this passage by saying,

"All these desires disquiet the soul and distract it from the peaceful quiet and sweet idleness of the contemplation which is being communicated to it."(47)

The second difficult passage is to be found in the **Ascent of Mount Carmel** where St. John is discussing the fittingness of leaving meditation for contemplation:

"For it must be known that the end of reasoning and meditation on the things of God is the gaining of some knowledge and love of God, and each time that the soul gains this through meditation, it is an act; and just as many acts, of whatever kind, end by forming a habit in the soul, just so, many of these acts of loving knowledge which the soul has been making one after another from time to time come through repetition to be so continuous in it that they become habitual."(48)

At first glance this text seems like it can be construed in the sense that the acts of loving knowledge appropriate to meditation form a habit of loving knowledge, which the soul exercises without the previous discursive acts as a kind of active contemplation. This interpretation is unfounded. The passage from acts of loving knowledge to the habit is not continuous in an ontological sense, but only in a chronological sense inasmuch as meditation provides the remote preparation for contemplation, not an intrinsic and essential one. St. John immediately points up this discontinuity by adding to the passage: "This end God is wont also to effect in many souls without the intervention of these acts (or at least without many such acts having preceded it), by setting them at once in contemplation." And he goes on to say that what was gained by meditation becomes "converted and changed into habit and substance of loving knowledge, of a general kind, and not distinct or particular as before", making it clear that the continuity between meditation and contemplation is not of an essential kind. The contemplation is infused contemplation and not an active kind that has grown out of the working of the faculties. This becomes abundantly clear when St. John continues this same passage:

"Wherefore, when it gives itself to prayer, the soul is now like one to whom water has been brought, so that he drinks peacefully, without labour, and is no longer forced to draw water through the aqueducts of past meditations and forms and figures. So that, as soon as the soul comes before God, it makes an act of knowledge, confused, loving, passive and tranquil, wherein it drinks of wisdom and love and delight."(49)

The reference here to St. Teresa is unmistakable and refers to what she called the prayer of quiet, and clearly indicates the infused nature of the contemplation.

The sense of this passage is further clarified when a few numbers further on St. John emphatically states, "when the contemplative has to turn aside from the way of meditation and reasoning, he needs this general and loving attentiveness or knowledge of God. The reason is that if the soul at this time had not this knowledge of God or this realization of His presence, the result would be that it would do nothing and have nothing."(50)

The third and final text comes from the **Living Flame of Love**:

"Since God, then, as giver, is communing with the soul by means of loving and simple knowledge, the soul must likewise commune with Him by receiving with a loving and simple knowledge or advertence, so that knowledge may be united with knowledge and love with love."(51)

When "the deep and delicate voice of God" is heard and "is conscious of being led into silence, and hearkens, it must forget even that loving advertence of which I have spoken, so that it may remain free for that which is then desired of it; for it must practice that advertence only when it is not conscious of being brought into solitude or rest or forgetfulness or attentiveness of the spirit, which is always accompanied by a certain interior absorption." (52)

The proper interpretation of this passage demands an examination of the context that it is imbedded in, as well as an appreciation of the nuances of what St. John means by loving attentiveness. In the number that precedes this passage he writes:

"For God secretly and quietly infuses into the soul loving knowledge and wisdom without any intervention of specific acts, although sometimes He specifically produces them in the soul for some length of time. And the soul has then to walk with loving advertence to God, without making specific acts, but conducting itself, as we have said, passively, and making no efforts of its own, but preserving this simple, pure and loving advertence, like one that opens his eyes with the advertence of love."(53)

LOVING ATTENTIVENESS

Loving attentiveness is a complex reality that consists of two interpenetrating dimensions. The primary dimension is the contemplative experience itself, or loving knowledge, as when St. John states:

"The soul is alone, with an attentiveness and a knowledge, general and loving, as we said, but without any particular understanding, and adverting not to that which it is contemplating."(54)

Loving knowledge as the designation for contemplation also appears in the two passages from the **Living Flame** that have just been cited.

The other dimension of loving attentiveness is the human response to the contemplative experience. This response has two modalities. The first is a loving advertence which occurs at the very beginning of contemplation when the contemplative is learning to turn from his discursive activity and tries to be receptive to the new experience that is welling up in him. This is a more conscious and deliberate attentiveness. The second aspect of this loving attentiveness is when the contemplation has succeeded in making itself felt, and then it should become more passive and unreflective, and thus St. John says in the **Living Flame** that loving advertence in the first sense must be forgotten when the contemplative experience makes itself more strongly felt. This advertence, however, cannot be separated from the actual beginning of contemplation. It is not a way to make a long journey to contemplation, but rather, to become aware of the contemplation that is already present. The more contemplation becomes manifest, the more the recipient has to be on guard against interposing its own specific acts between himself and the contemplative experience, and even against trying to maintain a distinct awareness of his own receptivity. With these points clearly in mind we are in a much better position to understand the changes that were introduced by the developers of acquired contemplation.

CHAPTER 5

ACQUIRED CONTEMPLATION IN THE 17TH CENTURY

Jung, accompanied by a peasant, once arrived at a large manor house in a horse-drawn wagon, and as they drove into the courtyard the gates flew shut and the peasant exclaimed, "Now we are caught in the 17th century."(1)

This was, of course, a dream, and it was years until Jung realized that it referred to alchemy which reached its height at this time and played a crucial role in his attempts to objectively validate his psychology. In alchemy's obscure symbolism he saw acted out the same psychological processes that he had discovered in his own life and those of his patients. It rescued him from being a solitary voice, and verified the universal nature of modern psychological experiences.

The 17th century was home, as well, to a whole school of spirituality which developed in part as a response to the writings of St. Teresa and St. John. Like alchemy it is obscure, hidden in the dust of history, and potentially significant. The story lies buried in rare volumes, unedited manuscripts and heated controversies that have long since faded from public view. In it the fortuitous marriage of great experience, keen intellect and practical intent that made St. John's writings so exceptional were succeeded by works of theological elaboration. The academic theology of the time was deployed not only to defend St. John from his detractors, but to attempt to assimilate this new understanding of contemplation by creating a multitude of distinctions.

The history of spirituality is not immune from the temptation to assume that the spiritual writers of the 17th century would, by the very fact of following St. John in time, develop and clarify the rich and complex teachings

that he left. It comes somewhat as a shock then, to discover that many of these treatises display a poor grasp
of St. John, and far from completing and developing him,
never attain his level. Further, as the fame of St. John
grows greater and greater, it becomes harder to realize
that during his life and immediately following his death
there was no unanimous opinion about the value of his
writings, even within the Carmelite Order.

The world of the practitioner of acquired contemplation
makes a striking contrast to that of the Alchemists. They
did not attempt to explore inner realities through the
medium of matter, but tried to live and describe the most
subtle and refined interior attitudes of prayer by which
they could become contemplatives and attain divine union.
These writers were not simply isolated specialists; standing
on the brink of the 17th century we are met with a world
that is slowly developing an enthusiasm for interior prayer
which will grow to such dimensions that it will appear to
the nervous authorites as a spiritual contagion that is
sweeping everything else before it.

The writings of St. John of the Cross were a vital
ingredient in creating a psychological climate in which
people were forced to consider whether they, personally,
were called to contemplation. If a person reads St. John
and feels called both within and by the very religious
community he lives in to a life of contemplation, yet does
not actually experience infused contemplation, then the
stage is set for him to discover another kind of contemplation which will allow him to be the contemplative he
so much wants to be. The writings of St. John inadvertently become the tinder waiting for the spark of acquired
contemplation. Once the spark was struck, it will seem an
obvious solution, and set off a brush fire of interest in
what became called not only acquired or active contemplation, but the prayer of simple regard, prayer of faith, etc.
And this interest was to culminate in the exaggerations
of Quietism, and when this conflagration burned down at
the end of the century, buried in the ashes of false mysticism was also much of the practical interest in genuine
mysticism. Even though it was inevitable that someone
would stumble on the idea of acquired contemplation, it
is fascinating and instructive to attempt to discover who
lit this fire.

THOMAS OF JESUS

In the year 1608 the first use of the words acquired contemplation appeared in a treatise called "A Brief Treatise of Affirmative and Negative Obscure Knowledge of God", which was included in a book by the Benedictine Antonio de Alvarado entitled **The Art of Living Well.** This created a puzzle for scholars in the first half of this century who were debating the origin of acquired contemplation. Some held that it was a work that should be attributed to St. John himself, while others felt Alvarado might have been the original author. The attribution of the book to St. John was hindered by the fact that his literary style was very different, and if it was actually the work of Alvarado, the mystery only deepened, for what was a Benedictine doing echoing St. John and developing this doctrine ten years before the publication of the first edition of St. John's writings?

There were, however, two notable early Carmelite spiritual writers standing in the wings that had made use of this term several years after it appeared in Alvarado's book: Thomas of Jesus, and John of Jesus and Mary (Calhorra). The mystery was not solved until after World War II when the Carmelite scholar, Fr. Simeon of the Holy Family, was browsing among the manuscripts of the National Library in Madrid. There he came across a spiritual treatise entitled, **The First Part of the Spiritual Path of Prayer and Contemplation** which was attributed to the Portuguese Carmelite Joseph of the Holy Spirit, but it did not seem to match Fr. Joseph's other works and was, in fact, much more reminiscent of the writings of Thomas of Jesus, and so after careful consideration Fr. Simeon came to the conclusion that:

"The **Brief Treatise of Obscure Knowledge of God** (Alvarado's treatise) is taken, in its major part, from the **Treatise of Contemplation** of Fr. Thomas of Jesus, contained in Book 3 of his **First Part of the Spiritual Path of Prayer and Contemplation.**"(2)

And he found that this treatise of contemplation which Thomas had included in his **First Part of the Spiritual Path:**

"had already existed in its primitive and independent form by the beginning of 1604, having been composed during the three or four first years that the founder

(Thomas of Jesus himself) of the Carmelite Deserts passed in the glorious solitude of Las Batuecas."(3)

Who, then, was this Thomas of Jesus? E. Allison Peers, the noted English expert on the history of Spanish mysticism, considered him the most interesting of the Carmelite spiritual writers in the post-Teresan period.(4) He had been born at Baeza in 1568 and was apparently a precocious student, for he gained a doctorate in law and one in theology before he joined the Carmelites in 1587. His rise in the Order was rapid, and by 1597 he was the Provincial of Old Castile. Fr. Thomas was a man of many parts, not only quick of intellect, but full of new ideas. He conceived of a scheme to create desert monasteries which would function as hermitages to allow the friars to replenish their energies in these isolated and quiet settings, and it was in the Desert of Las Batuecas that he probably composed most of his major spiritual works, even though some were not printed until much later. It was also Thomas of Jesus, together with John of Jesus and Mary (Aravalles), who was appointed by the Chapter General of the Reform held in September, 1601, "to examine and approve" the works of John of the Cross so they could be printed.(5) Two years later the matter was left in the hands of Thomas of Jesus alone.

If Thomas was interested in hermitages, he was equally fascinated by the missions, and received an invitation to go to the Congo as Papal Ambassador. In 1607 he was secretly summoned by the Pope to Rome, and though his trip to the Congo never materializaed, he soon immersed himself in schemes for the development of the missions. He tried to found a congregation of Carmelites that would be a completely missionary one. Though this scheme never reached fruition, he published an enormous work on the missions which included sections of the evangelization of Greeks, Jews, Moslems, pagans and heretics.(6) In 1610 he was sent by the Pope to the Low Countries where he founded a whole series of monasteries. He continued with this active and strenuous work until his health gave way and he died in Rome in 1627.

An air of mystery surrounds Thomas of Jesus' relationship with St. John. Here is a man who had joined the Carmelite Order before the death of St. John and who might have known him earlier as a student in Baeza when John was the rector of the Carmelite House of Studies there, but cannot be classified as a simple disciple. For example, Thomas never cited St. John in his printed works, even when it was a question of his major treatises on contemplation where such citations would seem appropriate. Nor did he cite St. John in the **First Part of the Spiritual Path** and in his treatise on acquired contemplation, even when he is following St. John's thoughts. At the same time, he had to be aware of St. John's writings through his commission to prepare them for publication and there is in existence, as we will see a little later, proof that he carefully considered these writings.(7)

Further, if Thomas held the commission to prepare St. John's writings for publication, why wasn't this project ever brought to fruition? He certainly had time and opportunity, for during this period he composed much of his literary production. And in fact, he actually did do the preparatory work, as a manuscript annotated by him shows. When St. John's work finally appeared in 1618, it was under the direction of Diego de Jesus (Salabanca) and contained many changes. Salabanca at one point had a close relationship with Thomas of Jesus, and towards the end of his life tried to mitigate his responsibility for these changes by claiming he made them under the orders of his superiors. Did Thomas of Jesus, in fact, have a hand in how the first edition appeared?

Finally, St. John's **Spiritual Canticle** was absent from the first edition, and is absent from the manuscript of John's writings that Thomas annotated. Jean Krynen has claimed that not only did the **Spiritual Canticle** appear in various places only after Thomas had left them, but that he rewrote the **Spiritual Canticle** on the basis of John's first version, and the commentaries of Antolinez.(8) All these puzzles have the cumulative effect of showing how problematical our knowledge of Fr. Thomas is, and it is in this context we should look at the question of the origin of his doctrine of acquired contemplation.

Thomas as an ascetical and mystical writer produced a whole series of treatises that range from a brief summary of St. Teresa's ideas on prayer to large treatises on contemplation. Some of this production was published during his lifetime, while others remained in manuscript until the 20th century, and still others, like the **First Part of the Spiritual Path**, remain unedited.

In his attempts to understand the nature of contemplation, he divides it into three different kinds.(9) The first is acquired contemplation, which, though it needs the ordinary support of grace, operates in a human mode and depends on the virtues. The second is infused contemplation which works through the influence of the Holy Spirit by means of His gifts. The third, which he called supereminent contemplation, and which was higher than infused contemplation, came about in the form of an immediate movement or illumination of God by means of a transient act that acted in a superhuman mode, and this last form of contemplation was not the development of the virtues or gifts, but a charism, a special grace freely given by God. Thomas felt that even though acquired contemplation depended in some way on the whole organism of the spiritual life, both virtues and the gifts of the Holy Spirit, as well, it differed from infused contemplation because in the latter there was some kind of experimental actuation of the gifts by which the soul felt a great facility in exercising prayer. Infused contemplation works above the ordinary course of grace to produce this facility in prayer under the experimental motion of the gifts of the Holy Spirit. In acquired prayer there is not this same experimental actuation. It remains latent, and the soul has to operate in the human mode. The highest form of contemplation, this supereminent one, consists of rapture, ecstasy and prophecy, as well as the experimental perception of God or mystical union, and this kind of prayer is rarely given, according to Thomas.

Thomas' principle treatments of acquired contemplation are to be found in the **First Part of the Spiritual Path** and in his **De Contemplatione Acquisita.** Fr. Simeon, considering Thomas' doctrine in the former, summarizes it as follows:

"To none of those who exercise themselves in prayer does Fr. Thomas exclude from being able to arrive at the contemplation of mystical theology...Some will enter in it passively and supernaturally lifted by God, others will enter with their industry and work, although supposing the ordinary divine concourse in the supernatural order."(10)

In addition to there being two classes, acquired and infused contemplation, Thomas finds two modes or manners of contemplation. One is affirmative and the other negative, and each of these can be either acquired or infused. (11) Affirmative contemplation goes from a knowledge of

creatures to a knowledge of God. But it is negative contemplation which, according to Thomas, is a higher state
that seems to capture most of his interest. He discovers
various grades of it, active and infused, but again his
attention is on the active, negative contemplation. In this
kind of contemplation the soul raises itself above all that
is sensible, imaginable or intelligible until its intelligence
comes to rest in the incomprehensibility of God, and finding itself in such an abyss the intellect loses its way, so
to speak, and the will is inflamed and loves that God
which cannot be known with particular and distinct knowledge. This, Thomas calls one of the grades of mystical
theology, or mysticism.

How does a person know that they should pass from
meditation to contemplation, or from the clear and distinct knowledge of affirmative contemplation to negative
contemplation? Thomas gives any number of signs which
echo St. John. For entering into contemplation one should
have practiced the purgative and illuminative ways, and
though it is difficult to give an exact time to be spent
in the way of meditation, Thomas mentions that after a
year of novitiate a person could be ready to move to
contemplation. In order to know the precise moment
Thomas gives further signs: an inability to meditate like
before, a distaste for meditation that doesn't proceed from
lukewarmness or negligence, the fact that during meditation the person has stopped with admiration or delight
upon seeing some truth, and finally, being unable to meditate, the person exercises himself in virtue and petition.
(12)

Even more interesting are the signs that Thomas gives
for entering into this negative contemplation, and it is
important to keep in mind that this negative contemplation
is Thomas' active, negative contemplation that does not
exclude anyone given the normal help of grace. The first
sign is that whatever the soul hears or understands by
means of the senses, whether of God or of creatures, does
not satisfy it, but rather is tedious to it. The second is
that it doesn't take any pleasure in anything it knows of
God or of creatures, and the third is that within itself it
feels a growing desire, hunger and thirst of God.

Since this is an active, negative contemplation Thomas
gives two means by which a person can actively enter into
it. The first way is by means of the understanding in

which a person goes from knowledge to knowledge until it comes to a negative knowledge by which it enters into the divine darkness, and then the will takes over, loving and enjoying God. The second way to enter into this contemplation is to close the eyes of the understanding, contenting ourselves with the knowledge we have by faith, and putting our effort into the acts of the will to which is granted what is not given to the understanding, and aspiring to God with lively desires to unite and join ourselves to Him. This, according to Thomas, the writers of mystical theology call travelling by faith.

After describing these ways to enter into contemplation, Thomas devotes himself to a discussion of the various means by which a person "is able to enter actively and progress in the exercise of the obscure contemplation".(13) Here the echoes of St. John grow louder and become almost a full-fledged paraphrasing of him. What is necessary is to denude oneself of all the vital operations of both the senses and the intellect, as well as the memory and the will. Every image and appetite of the creature must be eliminated because it cannot serve as a proportionate means of union with God. This emptying out of all the things that have entered the senses or the higher powers is to bring a person as close as possible to the purity in which they were created, and here Thomas evokes the image of the tabula rasa. All the sense impressions and distinct kinds of knowledge that come from the intellect, memory and will have to be emptied out, for they are not proportionate to God. This process of emptying starts with the senses and moves to the intellect, and Thomas goes on in the rest of the treatise describing the purification of the intellect, memory and will, which parallels St. John's **Ascent.**

All this shows a concentrated reading of St. John. Yet, if we penetrate beyond these surface similarities, we are confronted with a world of thought that has departed significantly from his doctrine. For St. John, the term "loving and general knowledge" always means, as we have seen, infused contemplation, but for Thomas it can mean a knowledge born of faith "which is no more than a knowledge of faith with which we know God as incomprehensible" and "contemplation is no other than a loving look at the truth..." and "the contemplation of mystical theology is...a burning and loving look at the incomprehensibility of God, which, because it does not fall under any particular knowledge of the understanding, is called general and confused knowledge." This kind of contemplation is quiet and peaceful because it does not attach itself to anything particular, and therefore is "so subtle and delicate that it is almost imperceptible."(14) But this imperceptibility does not arise from the fact that the infused prayer is by-passing the faculties, but it is a result of the active process of negation that has left aside all particular perceptions.

In a similar way, if loving attentiveness is never separated by St. John from the actual reception of contemplation, for Thomas its meaning is transformed into an active exercise of particular acts which lead it to acquire a habit of contemplation, and each of these acts "is no more than a burning desire of love to join itself with this God which it knows by faith". In this kind of contemplation the soul recognized that God is beyond all the attributes that can be attributed to Him. It understands that God is incomprehensible and so it contemplates the incomprehensibility of God by faith, and exercises this faith "together with a burning desire to penetrate and unite itself with God in a manner that, when this general and confused knowledge, which by means of faith we have of God is exercised habitually, together with love, it comes to be the contemplation of mystical theology".(15)

It is important to realize that Thomas is not talking about an actual experience of infused contemplation. There is no perceptible experience, no loving infusion, but simply acts of faith and love. We recognize God transcends all our perceptions of Him, yet we take up an attitude of belief in Him and desire to be united with Him. Thus, logically, if we call this contemplation, it is a contemplation that can be exercised whenever we want to.

The themes that occupied Thomas in the **Spiritual Path** were of enduring interest to him. Towards the end of his life, sometime between the close of 1622 and 1627, he wrote his scholastic style treatise entitled **De Contemplatione Acquisita**. In it Thomas defines acquired contemplation as: "An affectionate and sincere knolwedge of God and His effects which is gained by our own industry".(16) Acquired contemplation is rowing the boat, while infused contemplation is having the wind fill the sails and drive it along.

This small book contains substantially the same doctrine as the **First Part of the Spiritual Path.** Thomas spends two chapters enumerating the signs for the passage from meditation to contemplaion. Again he mentions that novices, after their year of training, are often ready for contemplation, and again he develops the theme of acquired contemplation hand-in-hand with references to infused contemplation. Among his signs for the transition to contemplation the following is the most certain: if someone, after having exercised themselves in meditation to good effect, finds a difficulty in meditating despite their efforts, it is a manifest sign that God is granting some grace of contemplation, although it is hidden. He goes on to refine this sign by referring to St. John's comments on melancholy or other humors of the mind and body.(17) Unfortunately, since Thomas' vocabulary is so reminiscent of St. John's, there is a grave danger that we will begin to confuse these two very different views of contemplation. St. John speaks only of infused contemplation and it will do violence to his writings to find in them an acquired kind, still less a supereminent degree.

But if Thomas is the first to talk of an active contemplation which did not exist in the writings of St. John, how did he come to create such a doctrine? The best supposition is that it emerged out of the circumstances of his own interior life. Thomas had been attracted to join the Carmelites because he read St. Teresa, and he was especially moved by her description of an intellectual vision of the Trinity. We have seen that Thomas was not the kind of man who would shrink from any goal he saw in front of himself. When he thought about the missions, it was in the context of actually going. If he read St. Teresa's descriptions of the wonderful graces of the interior life, he would do everything in his power to attain them. He joined the Carmelites, he devoted himself to the study of St. Teresa's and St. John's writings, and he conceived the idea to found the Carmelite deserts. It is not unthinkable that this latter project came as the exterior effect of this attempt to do everything in his power to prepare himself for the contemplative life.

But Thomas' pursuit of these interior goals had a very strong intellectual coloring. He wanted to put the mystical sciences on a solid basis of theological scholarship. He felt that supernatural contemplation was rarely understood because of the obscure and symbolic language in which spiritual people spoke of it. If he could clarify it, it would be more accessible to everyone, and he leaves us a crucial fact about his own interior life. He tells us he had no experience of contemplation, but after twenty years of attempting to understand it God opened His hand and made him understand the nature of this union, and this gave him the hope that he could inspire his neighbor by describing these heavenly riches.

If we understand Thomas' twenty years loosely, and date them from his university studies in Baeza prior to his entrance into the Carmelites in 1587, then this burst of understanding coincides with his time in Las Batuecas when he composed most of his major spiritual treatises, including the **First Part of the Spiritual Path.** It also coincides with the time he was "examining and approving" the writings of St. John in order to prepare them for publication. Thus, at the very time he is attempting to live out the contemplative life in an especially intense way and, no doubt, dealing with the questions and problems of the friars living with him, he is also engaged in a study of John of the Cross, and out of this combination of circumstances emerged the doctrine of acquired contemplation.

Looking at it from the human point of view, if anyone ought to have been a contemplative, it was Thomas of Jesus, but since he never received any contemplative experience, this desire for contemplation expressed itself in a reinterpretation of St. John and the construction of another kind of contemplation open to everyone who is willing to labor for it. As Krynen put it, "The very notion of acquired contemplation translates on the doctrinal plane the sustained and unfruitful effort of Thomas of Jesus to arrive at living and understanding the mystical experience itself."(18)

This reconstruction of the events that surrounded Thomas of Jesus' creation of acquired contemplation is strengthened by another discovery of the industrious Fr. Simeon. This time, while sifting through the archives of the International Carmelite College in Rome, he discovered an early manuscript of St. John's writings that had been annotated by Thomas. The elaborate title that this manuscript bore led him to conclude that it might have been prepared by Thomas during his labors that were supposed to lead to the first edition of St. John's writings, and a careful examination of the manuscript made him place the various marks and marginal notes in it sometime between the year 1601 and 1603.(19)

What we possess, then, is a way in which to see into Thomas' mind and determine what aspects of St. John's writings preoccupied him at this time, and what immediately leaps out at us is his concern with the passages that have to do with the transition to contemplation. For example, he makes a line in the margin for the passage in the **Dark Night** where St. John is describing the second sign, which we have seen is equivalent to the third in the **Ascent,** which is the actual infusion of contemplation and reads:

"...it (the soul) feels that it is deriving strength and energy to act from the substance which this inward food gives it, the which food is the beginning of a contemplation that is dark and arid to the senses; which contemplation is secret and hidden from the very person that experiences it; and ordinarily, together with the aridity and emptiness which it causes in the senses, it gives the soul an inclination and desire to be alone and in quietness..." (20)

In this passage he also underlines the phrase starting from "from the substance" down to "together with", and thus is bracketing the very significant phrase, "which contemplation is secret and hidden from the very person that experiences it." He takes note of the three temptations on the road to contemplation which have already caught our attention, and via marginal signs, signals his interest in that troublesome passage in the **Dark Night:**

"They must be content simply with a loving and peaceful attentiveness to God, and live without the anxiety, without the effort, and without the desire to taste or feel Him. All these desires disquiet the soul and distract it from the peaceful quiet and sweet idleness of the contemplation which is being communicated to it."(21)

This passage appears to have captured Thomas' attention more than any other. Opposite it in the large margin he places his longest note, unfortunately cut by the binder's knife, and he underlines "without the desire to", and he also apparently makes an addition to the text by adding between the lines the word "mucho" after "without" and on top of "anxiety".

These indications of interest on Thomas' part can be

understood as a preoccupation about this critical moment
of transition, and they represent the vast proportions of
the annotations that Thomas made on this manuscript.

There is perhaps a more nuanced explanation for the
emergence of acquired contemplation out of the life of
Thomas of Jesus. Instead of Thomas simply lacking contemplative experience, and thus fashioning a parallel to
infused contemplation out of the culmination of meditation, his actual experience of contemplation might have
been of a reality that fell between these two poles. The
life of prayer in such an energetic personality could have
culminated in the development of the active gifts of the
Holy Spirit, and as a consequence Thomas could have
experienced contemplation in a masked form which would
have lent a contemplative savor to affective prayer and
the practice of the presence of God. In such a case the
contemplation which is simply the fruit of meditation
would be experienced as if it were actually the beginning
of infused contemplation. Yet, his doctrine, when read and
practiced without a similar activation of these gifts, would
blossom with consequences that could have been held in
check in Thomas' own case.(22)

CHANGES IN THE 1ST EDITION

It was not until 27 years after St. John's death that
his works were finally printed. This was approximately 15
years after Thomas of Jesus' writings on acquired contemplation, and 10 years after part of that work had appeared
under Antonio de Alvarado's name in 1608. The many
changes that existed in the first edition, as well as the
omission of the **Spiritual Canticle**, must be seen against
the background of the greater editorial license exercised
in those times, and the desire of the Carmelite authorities
to protect these writings from charges of Illuminism. They
attempted to soften the sharp distinctions that St. John
made between active prayer and the passive infused nature
of contemplation. And they do something else as well; they
help smooth the way for the propagation of acquired contemplation.

Critical Edition   First Edition

Although, as we have said,

Critical Edition	First Edition
the soul in this state of knowledge believes itself to be doing nothing, and to be entirely unoccupied, because it is working neither with the senses nor with the faculties, it should realize that it is not wasting time.(23)	...it should realize that it is not wasting time, nor acting uselessly.
In order to reach this state, (contemplation) it will frequently need to make use of meditation, quietly and in moderation; but, when once **the soul is brought into this other state, it acts not at all with its faculties.**(24)	but when once **this is attained, the soul neither reflects nor labours with** its faculties.
Wherefore in this state the soul must never have meditation imposed upon it, nor **must it make any acts,** nor strive after sweetness or fervor.(25)	meditation imposed upon it, nor **any acts produced by means of reflection,** nor strive knowingly after sweetness or fervour.
Causing the **natural** acts of their faculties to fail. (26)	Causing the **discursive** acts of their faculties to fail.
For not all those who walk of set purpose in the way of the spirit are brought by God to **contemplation, nor even the half of them-** why, He best knows.(27)	are brought by God to **perfect contemplation,-why** He best knows.

Attempts of this sort, while trying to shield St. John from charges of Illuminism, have the unfortunate consequence of attenuating his thought and making the reader wonder whether there is, indeed, some kind of natural act

that exists between meditation and infused contemplation.
This problem becomes more acute when it is a question
of loving attentiveness itself.

Critical Edition   First Edition

And the soul has then to
walk with loving advertence
to God, without making   loving advertence to God,
specific acts, but conducting   without performing any other
itself, as we have said,   specific acts than those to
passively, and making no   which it feels that He is
efforts of its own, but pre-   inclining it, but conducting
serving this simple, pure and   itself, as it were, passively.
loving advertence, like one
that opens his eyes with the
advertence of love.(28)

When this comes to pass,
and the soul is conscious of
being led into silence, and
hearkens, it must forget   and hearkens, even the lov-
even that loving advertence   ing awareness of which I
of which I have spoken, so   have spoken must be most
that it may remain free for   pure, without any anxiety
that which is then desired   or reflection, so that the
of it.(29)   soul almost forgets it
                                through being wholly occu-
                                pied in hearing, in order
                                that it may remain free for
                                that which is then desired
                                of it.

If those souls to whom this
comes to pass knew how to
be quiet at this time, and
troubled not about perform-   and troubled not about per-
ing any kind of action,   forming any kind of action,
whether inward or outward,   which they strive with their
neither had any anxiety   labour and their reasoning
about doing anything, then   to perform and had no
they would delicately experi-   anxiety to do anything save
ence this inward refreshment   to allow themselves to be
in that ease and freedom   led by God, to receive and

Critical Edition	First Edition
from care.(30)	to listen with loving interior attentiveness, then they would delicately experience...
And thus, when the soul desires to remain in inward ease and peace, any operation and affection or attention wherein it may then seek to indulge will distract it and disquiet it...(31)	any operation and affection or anxious attention...
the faculties are at rest, and are working, not actively, but passively, by receiving that which God works in them; and, if they work at times, it is not with violence or with carefully elaborated meditation, but with the sweetness of love, loved less by the ability of the soul itself than by God.(32)	the faculties are at rest and work not, save in that simple and sweet loving attentiveness; and if at times they work more it is not with violence

There is a tendency, then, in the first edition, to change the idea of loving attentiveness in the direction of making it a separate active operation. These amended texts could then become points of crystallization of a doctrine of acquired contemplation in an atmosphere that was already prone to interpret St. John in this way.

Acquired contemplation was not a development of St. John's teaching on the transition from meditation to contemplation, but rather it was a response to the challenge this teaching posed. If Thomas of Jesus was the first to formulate this kind of explanation, the very possibility of it was in the air he breathed. The problem of the transition to contemplation and the dark night had existed before him, for John carefully notes it and, no doubt, it had existed in various forms for a long time. This very real problem created the psychological climate in which a doctrine like acquired contemplation would become almost inevitable. Historical questions about its origin dwindle in significance as we realize that this whole inner atmosphere was urging men in this same direction and could have multiple points of development. Once the actual formulation of the doctrine of acquired contemplation was articulated, it would spread with great rapidity, and its very extensiveness, as well as its supposed relationship to St. John's writings, would become arguments in favor of its validity.

THE DIFFUSION OF ACQUIRED CONTEMPLATION

It is possible that Thomas was responsible for the spread of acquired contemplation within his order. This can be seen from the little we know about his relationships with John of Jesus and Mary (Calhorra) and José de Jesús María (Quiroga).

John of Jesus and Mary, although a Spaniard, lived his religious life among the Italian Carmelites and appeared to have no knowledge of St. John's work. He wrote a number of spiritual treatises, and his **School of Prayer**, first published in Rome in 1610, mentions the notion of acquired contemplation. This is the same place and date of Thomas' **Suma**, which also mentions acquired contemplation. Apparently they were both collaborating during these years on the idea of the Carmelite Missionary congregation, and they cite each other in their written works with approval. If John of Jesus and Mary did not know St. John's writings, and acquired contemplation was supposed to be a development of these writings, how could he have arrived at this notion? Could Thomas, arriving in Rome, having already worked out these ideas, communicated them to him?

Quiroga (1562-1628) is recognized as the other principle proponent and expounder of acquired contemplation in the early part of the 17th century. In his **Don Que Tuvo**, written between 1618 and 1628, he asserts that while God gave the Carmelite Order St. Teresa to teach them about infused contemplation, He gave them John of the Cross to instruct them in acquired contemplation.

What was the relationship between Thomas and Quiroga? Quiroga had become the historiographer general of the Carmelites in 1597. It would be surprising if they had not conferred during the years when Thomas was preparing St. John's writings for publication. Quiroga, in fact, had made a special effort to inform himself about St. John, and wrote a biography of him. But did Quiroga get the idea of acquired contemplation from Thomas and then clothe it in his own vocabulary? It is difficult to say.(33) There are apparent echoes of Thomas in the **Don Que Tuvo** when he describes an infused contemplation "of greater illumination than the gift of wisdom" which he contrasts to an acquired one exercised in the human mode "by a superintellectual concept" formed in the obscurity of faith.(34)

It is interesting to note that Quiroga gives us an example of how the changes in the first edition were immediately taken up in the formulation of the doctrine of acquired contemplation. Right after expounding these two kinds of contemplations Quiroga continues his apologia in order to defend St. John against the complaints that have arisen that in contemplation there is a cessation of particular acts. Here he quotes the first edition where it says, "the faculties are at rest and work not, save in that simple and sweet loving attentiveness". And thus he is equating this passage with his acquired contemplation, a task which would have been made much more difficult if he had had the original reading before him, which said: "The faculties are at rest, and are working, not actively, but passively, by receiving that which God works in them."

It would be an oversimplification to imagine that the doctrines on prayer that appeared in the 17th century could be understood simply as various reactions to St. John and St. Teresa. But this remains a valuable perspective not only for organizing the scattered information that is available, but for trying to make this information relevant to the practical problems that contemplation faces today. If various currents of what was labeled Illuminism existed in the time of St. Teresa and St. John, similar trends existed after them, and they could have played a role in the wide acceptance that acquired contemplation received and helped transform the way it had existed in the earliest Carmelite writers. In 1605, for example, Ana of Jesus, the talented spiritual daughter of St. Teresa, and the recipient of St. John's **Spiritual Canticle**, was in France working to establish the first Carmelite convent there. In a letter to an unknown person she writes: "I have care that the novices consider and imitate Our Lord Jesus Christ; because here He is often little remembered. Everything is a simple view of God; I don't know how this is able to be. Since the sojourn of the glorious St. Denis who wrote the mystical theology all the world has continued to apply itself to God by suspension rather than by imitation. That is a strange manner of proceding; in truth, I don't understand it..."(35)

Such a tendency, which seems as if it could have had little to do with Thomas of Jesus' articulation of acquired contemplation, would not only have a predilection for the writings of pseudo-Dionysius, as Thomas did himself, but would tend to interpret St. John's passage to contemplation as a more explicit exposition of these same ideas. The Illuminists of Seville in the 1620s made use of St. John's writings,(36) while their French counterparts availed themselves of those of Benoit de Canfield(37) without totally neglecting St. John. Thus, St. John's explanations of contemplation stimulated already existing currents of thought.

ANTONIO ROJAS

A second stage in the development of acquired contemplation can be dated to the late 1620s in Madrid, and its principle proponents were Antonio de Rojas and Juan Falconi. In 1628 Rojas published his **Life of the Spirit in Order to Know How to Have Prayer and Union With God.** This book, while being popular as indicated by the frequency it was reprinted, had no pretensions of originality, and would have faded from the history of spirituality if not for two events. One was its appreciative use of Augustine Baker, whose writings were edited into a manual of the spiritual life entitled **Holy Wisdom,** and from there exerted an influence on the practice of prayer down to our own time. The other event was the condemnation of Rojas' book because one of the censures was written by John of St. Thomas, the noted Dominican theologian whose works are still read today. It was the Carmelite scholar Eulogio Pacho who not only unearthed John of St. Thomas' opinion, but provides the information about Rojas' now almost inaccessible volume.(38)

The **Life of the Spirit** recommends a prayer of faith which is a simple gaze at God and a resting in Him that leaves aside all discourse and images. In substance it appears the same as that recommended by Thomas of

Jesus, but there is an insistence on the central role that this prayer should play in the spiritual life, and its efficacy that is characteristic of this later stage of development, as we will see when we look at the writings of Juan Falconi. The early Carmelite authors were too close to the writings of St. John and St. Teresa to avoid speaking at length about infused contemplation, but the implications of their doctrine of active contemplation now began to surface. Since St. John was made the father of acquired contemplation, then all the characteristics that he attributes to infused contemplation will gradually become attached to this prayer of faith. On the practical plane it will absorb infused contemplation and masquerade as the culmination of the spiritual life, and it will do all this while evoking the name of John of the Cross.

Rojas, for example, in all honesty could not understand the reasons for his condemnation. His book appeared with all sorts of recommendations and approvals by theologians and ecclesiastical authorities, and the "acquired supernatural contemplation" that he proposed was not only a way to exercise all the virtues, but this whole teaching was, as he states in the defense of the book he submitted to the Inquisition, "a compendium and a quintessence of what Padre Fray Juan de la Cruz wrote in the **Dark Night.**" In this same defense, he cites numerous spiritual authors whom he supposes held the same doctrine, but St. John holds a special place. He is cited explicitly when it is a question of the three signs, he is cited without attribution, and his thoughts are summarized. Among the other authors Rojas called to his defense are Quiroga in his **Life of St. John,** Antonio Alvarado's **The Art of Living Well,** and John of Jesus and Mary whom he mistakenly calls Gracian, leaving us to wonder whether he meant Aravalles or Calhorra.

In fact, it was his extensive use of St. John's doctrine that caused some of his initial problems. A Discalced Carmelite from Granada, Fr. Augustine of St. Joseph, read it and denounced it to the Inquisition as damaging to St. John's memory. Among his accusations he strikes at its oversimplification of the spiritual life by calling it a "stair without steps, a destination without a road to it, and an end without means",(39) and feels that this effort to pray without thinking will succeed if only because the person attempting it will be sleeping and dreaming. He approaches the heart of the real difficulty by discussing St. John's teaching of how to go from "meditation to infused contemplation". And he insists that if the three signs are not present, then one must remain in meditation, for not all receive this contemplation, and he complains that Rojas is not teaching the same doctrine.

The opinions of the original examiners of the Inquisition were divided, and the definitive statement was made by John of St. Thomas whose principle objection was that "after making an act of faith", Rojas taught "all discourse, images and imaginations of all created things should be left aside, keeping the understanding without discourse, thought or knowledge, as a dead person in God".(40) This the learned Dominican considered impossible to human nature, and though there were high spiritual states which transcended these natural means, they did not have to do with the kind of contemplation which was possible on our own initiative and which this book described. In essence, he hammers away at the lack of psychological realism that exists when attitudes suitable for infused prayer are taken up without this gift.

JUAN FALCONI

Juan Falconi, 1596-1638, was active in Madrid with an extensive ministry of spiritual direction during the years Rojas' **Life of the Spirit** appeared and came to grief. He wrote a number of treatises and letters on the spiritual life, most of which were not published during his lifetime. It is his **Letter to a Religious,** dated July 25, 1629, though it now only exists in an Italian translation (1674), that is particularly interesting for understanding Falconi's interpretation of John of the Cross. This letter is a defense against the complaints Falconi had received from a Discalced Carmelite about the type of prayer he was teaching. It has been suggested that the Carmelite was Fr. Augustine of St. Joseph whom we saw earlier denouncing Rojas.(41)

Falconi takes a particular interest in St. John's transition from meditation to contemplation:

"When it is time to pass to contemplation, I tell them to do it after this manner. They are to place themselves in the presence of God, believing God to be present and imminent everywhere. They must have a general notice of living faith, and resign themselves into His hands...And if, further, they are troubled by aridity and temptations, and think they are doing nothing, let them hold still to their faith and resignation without discourse or meditation so- ever. For this is contemplation, - that is to say, a simple and pure regard of the object."(42)

According to Falconi, it is time to exercise this con- templation when the savor of meditation has been lost, and this contemplation is "a general knowledge of lively faith in the presence of God"(43), and if anybody is to complain that this is doing nothing, Falconi refutes them by quoting St. John's remarks from the **Dark Night.**

With Falconi the reinterpretation of St. John's infused contemplation into an acquired one has reached its fullest development. As E. Allison Peers puts it,

"It is this contemplation which he (Falconi) substitutes for the whole extent of mystic experience higher than meditation, for all St. Teresa's inner Mansions and the higher slopes of St. John of the Cross' Mount Carmel. And apparently it gives him perfect and complete satisfac- tion."(44)

And Falconi, drawing out the consequences implicit in this position, asserts that this contemplation is a suitable exercise for all Christians.

"If they mean that it is not for all to pass to contem- plation after attaining to meditation, then are they greatly deceived...If a man has passed through meditation, he will be ripe for contemplation, and for so long as he is in that state he must know no other than the simple regard of living faith without reasoning or meditation or reflec- tion."(45)

In other writings, Falconi takes up themes that were to become important during the Quietist controversies towards the end of the century. This act of faith in which contemplation consists will endure unless it is consciously revoked: "For the soul to be in true prayer all the time... there is no need for it to be all the time attentive to God nor to be ever thinking upon Him. It suffices that at the beginning of thy prayer thou have such attention..."(46) And when this contemplation is pure, it is:

"so inward, and so spiritual, that it is scarcely noticed. It consists in placing oneself in the presence of God with a secret, intimate, and imperceptible intention and desire in the soul, to remain ever in His Hands and so to continue the loving surrender which it has made of itself to Him. And this it does by the very act of placing itself in His presence, without having any need of making any other sensible act, beyond that of placing itself before Him..." (47)

This passage echoes the **Ascent of Mount Carmel**, but gives a completely different meaning to it. Falconi's view of human nature would be just as objectionable to John of St. Thomas as Rojas' was. The normal human working of the faculties is suppressed with the hope that the distillation of this process of suppression and simplification will lead to a more spiritual act, and this supposed act is called contemplation and is endowed with all the qualities that St. John found in the experience of infused contemplation. It is even given qualities that transcend infused contemplation itself. It is a human fabrication of what contemplation ought to be like pushed to its ultimate limits. The very lack of experience is transformed into a guarantee of the sublime spiritual nature of what is transpiring even though it is neither conscious nor perceptible.

AUGUSTINE BAKER, 1575-1641

In the year 1605, while Thomas of Jesus was elaborating his ideas on acquired contemplation in solitude, Augustine Baker, an English convert to Catholicism, was attempting to struggle through his novitiate with the Benedictines in Padua. After three months of meditation, he found himself suffering from that difficult time of the decline of sensible fervor. He writes of himself:

"But at the end of that time, being now become ripe for a more pure and perfect prayer of the will, but neither in books nor by any instructions finding any directions thereunto, his recollection which had been formerly profound became much distracted, and his heart cold, dry and void of all good affections. Upon this change he endeavoured to stir up devotion by means of all the ways and means he could, seeking out the most moving books and pictures he could hear of; but all in vain. No working of the imagination or understanding could any longer produce any effect upon the will. Hereby it came to pass that his recollections were now so full of aridities and distractions and became so burdensome to him that he had not the courage or patience to continue them, but giving over mental prayer he contented himself with his vocal prayers and exterior observances, the virtue of which in a condition of so great solitude was so small (as to the working a good disposition in the soul) that he found a manifest decay in piety and all internal virtues, so that in a short time he became wholly tepid and extroverted." (48)

This state of spiritual perplexity was one of the factors that led him to leave the novitiate and return home to England. Baker eventually became a Benedictine priest, made what he called two other conversions to the spiritual life, and found books that held, he felt, the solution to the problem he had faced during his novitiate. One of these books was Antonio Rojas' **Life of the Spirit,** and Rojas' ideas on active contemplation were taken up by Baker and incorporated in the post-humus compilation of Baker's writings called **Holy Wisdom.**

Baker describes Rojas' method of prayer:

"as a prayer of internal silence, quietness, and repose. There is no meditation, nor even express direct acts of the will. It is a virtual, habitual loving attention to God rather than a formal direct tending to Him."(49)

And he goes on:

"Thus the soul with silent attention regards God alone; she rejects the images of all objects whatever; she frames no particular requests, nor makes express acts towards God; but remains in an absolute silence of tongue and thought with a sweet, tacit consent of love in the will, permitting God to take entire possession of her soul as of a temple wholly belonging and consecrated to Him."(50)

In Baker's mind this kind of prayer would grow more and more pure and spiritual, and the operations less perceptible until it brought the soul to the prayer of quiet, of which it was an imperfect imitation.(51)

Implicit in this kind of prayer is the same view of human nature that emerged in Rojas and Falconi. Taking up a thought that can be found in Falconi's **Letter to a Religious,** Baker says:

"Lastly, the soul has no fear that this respectful silence is mere idleness; she knows it is the effect of love and respect. Indeed, an intellectual soul is all activity, so that it cannot continue a moment without some desires. If, then, she rejects all desire for created objects, she cannot but tend inwardly in her affections towards God; it was for this purpose that she placed herself in a posture of prayer. Her tending to God is much like the flight of an eagle. After a few vigorous flaps of the wings, it extends them, and by virtue of its first efforts it continues its flight for some distance with great swiftness, yet with as much stillness and ease as if it were reposing in its nest."(52)

Baker's use of Rojas forms but one strand of his writings about contemplation, but it illustrates his tendency to devote a great deal of effort in describing the stages of the spiritual life that exist between meditation and infused contemplation, for example, what he called forced immediate acts, and a further stage called aspirations.

Though he had some knowledge of John of the Cross and St. Teresa, his understanding of infused contemplation was defective, and his own experience of it doubtful.(53) Though these various interior acts were supposed to lead to infused contemplation, this was more a hopeful theory than a reflection of personal experience. Baker describes himself lying in his bed for hours at a time exercising his will and feeling the working of this prayer in different parts of his body. "For half a year together his evening's exercise (not his morning's) had those motions, and the motions were very strong and violent...our scholar living alone was and might be loud enough in his voice, uttering and venting forth his fore-said senseless aspirations, yet not so but that he was sometimes in peril to have been heard by others, and if he had been heard or seen, he would doubtless have been adjudged for a man who were out of his wits."(54)

This bit of autobiography is not produced to belittle a man who was not only sincere, but talented, and whose writings have been an aid for many people in the development of their spiritual life, yet as a doctrine of acquired contemplation became more explicit, and its practice more intense, its psychic repercussions became more visible. This process is especially evident in the life of Miguel Molinos.

MIGUEL MOLINOS

Since Molinos has the reputation of being the most infamous of the Quietists, a natural reaction on first picking up his **Spiritual Guide** would be to expect it to be a compendium of the most glaring kind of spiritual errors.

Instead we read:

"There are two ways of approaching God, the one by consideration and discursive thought, and the other by pure faith, and indistinct, general and confused knowledge. The first is called meditation, the second internal recollection, or acquired contemplation."(55)

And what is this acquired contemplation?

"When the soul already knows the truth (either by a habit acquired through reasoning, or because the Lord hath given her particular light) and fixes the eyes of the mind on the demonstrated truth, beholding it sincerely in quietness and silence, without requiring considerations, reasonings or other proofs in order to be convinced, and when the will loves the truth, admiring and delighting itself therein, then this properly is called the prayer of faith, and prayer of rest, internal recollection or contemplation."(56)

In short, we are still very much in the world of acquired contemplation that has become familiar to us through men like Rojas and Falconi. In fact, before Molinos arrived in Rome in 1664, one of Falconi's works had already been published in Italian, and if we credit an anonymous biography of Molinos, he constantly spoke of Juan Falconi and recommended the reading of his **Letter to a Religious.** There was, apparently, a more or less developed interest in these kinds of interior prayer that he tapped and later dominated. Molinos became the best-known spiritual director of the Holy City, and when his **Spiritual Guide** was published in 1675, it appeared with numerous ecclesiastical recommendations. It was not until ten years later that Molinos was arrested as a consequence of the discovery of a private teaching, and imprudent and immoral conduct. All the propositions of his condemnation stemmed from this private teaching rather than his published writings.

If Molinos had a predilection for Falconi's **Letter to a Religious,** he was also acquainted with the writings of John of the Cross. Though he does not cite him explicitly in the **Spiritual Guide,** the rhythms of St. John's writings are clear enough.

"As often as the end is obtained, the means cease, and when the ship arrives in the harbour the voyage is over. So if the soul after she hath wearied herself by means of meditation, shall arrive at the stillness, tranquility, and rest of contemplation, she ought then to put an end to all discursive thought, and repose in loving contemplation and simple vision of God, seeing and loving Him, gently rejecting all the images of Him that present themselves, calming the mind in that Divine Presence, collecting the memory, and fixing it wholly on God, contenting herself with the general and vague knowledge, which she has of God by means of faith, with all the force of the will loving Him in whom rests all fruition."(57)

But at the same time the misunderstandings of the nature of the contemplation described by St. John that existed in Falconi are taken up by Molinos. And when he comes to the question of the signs that indicate the proper time to pass to contemplation, he is naturally talking about acquired contemplation, and instead of three signs, he gives five:

1. an inability to meditate that does not come from natural disinclination, lack of preparation or melancholy. This is "the first and chief".

2. The soul seeks solitude and avoids conversation.

3. "that the reading of Godly books is usually tedious, because they speak not of the internal sweetness that rests in the heart, though it be not recognized."

4. "though the soul finds herself deprived of discursive thought yet does she firmly purpose to persevere in prayer."

5. "that she will experience a great knowledge of herself, abhorring her sins, and perceiving better the holiness of God."(58)

Unless we read a great deal into sign three, we will notice that St. John's chief sign, which is the actual experience of contemplation is missing, and the sign that seems to take predominance is the first. Given a failure of discursive thought, the soul should be taught by an experienced director how to take up this prayer of faith or this internal recollection. This inability to meditate "is a clear sign, that the Lord will have thee to walk by faith and silence in his Divine Presence, which is the most profitable and the easiest path; because with a simple vision of God, and with loving intentness on Him, the soul appears like a humble supplicant before her Lord..."(59)

The parallels between St. John and Molinos could be drawn out at great length,(60) and they seem to indicate more than an indirect knowledge of St. John's writings.

This impression is confirmed by a manuscript that exists in the Vatican Library dating from 1680 called **Defensa de la Contemplación** which was Molinos' reply to the critics of the **Spiritual Guide**. In it, like Rojas before him, he asserts that he is teaching what St. John taught and cites the mystical doctor in detail. A comparison of this defense with the **Spiritual Guide** leads to the conclusion that Molinos knew St. John's works directly at the time he composed this work. But as in the case of Thomas of Jesus, we are left with the mystery of why he never publicly cited him.

Molinos also took up Falconi's doctrine of the duration of the contemplative act unless consciously revoked, and he points out in the **Spiritual Guide** that the soul that takes up the attitude of internal recollection will suffer all sorts of assaults from the enemy. During the preceedings of the Holy Office his ideas on non-resistance to diabolical temptations in the lower part of the soul while engaged in the prayer of contemplation weighed heavily against him. As Ronald Knox puts it:

"Curiously, the only condemned propositions which are textual are also the most damning ones. It appears that at some stage in his examination Molinos actually asked to have a memorandum of his own incorporated in the findings of the Inquisitors; and this is represented (possibly in full) by propositions 41-53, which deal with temptations of the devil, and the reasons for not resisting them in our times of prayer."(61)

In a twisted and distorted way Molinos attempted to integrate these temptations of sense which were probably accentuated by his inner attitude into the life of prayer and give them a positive meaning. They were still the work of the devil, but the superior part of the soul remained undisturbed and did not need to do anything about them or feel guilty even if the physical body committed some impure act, for God used these means to humble and purify it. Since the acquired contemplation of Molinos is modeled after infused contemplation, there is a tendency to insist on the duration of the act of faith as if this act had a perceptible object in a manner analogous to the actual experience of infused contemplation itself. If a person tried to maintain an attentiveness without it having a perceptible object, they produce a psychological vacuum in consciousness, which manifestations of psychic energy out of the unconscious attempt to fill. From a psychological point of view it is not surprising to find these extreme forms of acquired contemplation linked with what appear to be autonomous motions in the lower part of the soul, that is, the unconscious, a theme that will be examined more closely in Chapter 7.

With Molinos' condemnation in 1685 and the censure of Madame Guyon after the controversies of Fenelon and Bousset in the last years of the century, the curtain rang down on the Quietist controversies. The five men that have been considered here, that is, Thomas of Jesus, Rojas, Falconi, Baker and Molinos, represent only one thread in the complex tapestry of the wide-spread interest in interior prayer that ran its course in these 100 years, and there are significant differences between them. Yet, as a group they shared a number of common characteristics. They were sincere, they read St. John of the Cross, and they had no actual experience of infused contemplation.(62) Thus, the personal spiritual circumstances of Thomas of Jesus were shared by all of them, and they found a solution in acquired contemplation. They took St. John's loving attentiveness which was the response to the actual experience of contemplation and made of it a separate active exercise of the soul.

By the end of the 17th century anti-mystical tendencies that had co-existed and interacted with these interests in interior prayer since before St. John's time, finally and definitively gain an upper hand. Aided by the exaggerations of Quietism they suppressed both genuine and spurious mysticism and created a climate of distrust that has lasted into the 20th century. Unwittingly, St. John's writings played a role in this tragedy.(63)

I will leave the story of acquired contemplation for the moment, but it is important to return to it later, for it contains not only an important caution on how not to understand St. John, but a hidden lesson of great significance for the life of prayer.

In summary, St. John's finely nuanced doctrine of the transition from meditation to contemplation should be carefully distinguished from the later interpretations of the various schools of acquired contemplation. With a clearer understanding of what contemplation meant to St. John we can turn to the question of the interaction between contemplation and individuation.

PART III

A PSYCHOLOGICAL LIGHT ON JOHN OF THE CROSS
AND THE LIFE OF PRAYER

CHAPTER 6

A TYPOLOGICAL PORTRAIT OF ST. JOHN

If we could assume that St. John's journey to contemplation and Jung's process of individuation were virtually identical and differed only in vocabulary, and because of the development of consciousness over the last 400 years, then we could simply discover in St. John another example of this universal psychic process. But if, as our discussion of Jung's empirical science and description of St. John's doctrine of contemplation seem to indicate, the issue is not so straightforward, then we face a much more difficult task.

There are many similarities between St. John and Jung, even profound affinities. Both men were engaged in the care of souls, and this preoccupation shaped their writings, and for both, an experience of God was at the root of their inner lives.

Yet the discontinuities are striking as well. Not only do they use different conceptual languages, and have different epistemological foundations, but the experiences of God they are talking about appear quite diverse. We do not have to attempt to reduce the contemplative life to an instance or example of the process of individuation. Nor do we have to decree a rather arbitrary solution to the question in which these two inner experiences would inhabit separate parts of the psyche, or one would begin where the other left off.

The approach that seems to do the least violence to both Jung and St. John is one in which these two processes are seen as essentially distinct in themselves, but intimately connected and vitally influencing each other in one, concrete, psyche. If we adopt this perspective, it does not mean that in actual fact, that is, in lived existence, the process of individuation is foreign to mystical experience, or vice versa. It is entirely possible that someone who is undergoing the process of individuation, especially when it is under the guise of a search for religious meaning, could experience aspects of St. John's journey to contemplation. Further, someone called to contemplation will almost inevitably be experiencing things that can best be explained in terms of Jung's psychology. It is this second possibility that we will explore in this chapter and the following one. The present chapter looks at St. John's life from the point of view of typology and the process of individuation, while the next looks at the transition to contemplation in the light of the dynamics of psychic energy.

PSYCHOLOGICAL TYPES

If we could understand both St. John's inner psychological development and the growth of his mystical life, we would be in a position on the practical level to understand something about the relationship between individuation and the contemplative life. Unfortunately, such a task is partially thwarted by St. John's passion for privacy, the lack of a distinctive psychological point of view in those days, and the demands of hagiography that turned his first biographers away from describing many of the human details that would be revelatory of his personality.

The basic biographical facts that do exist have been carefully sifted and presented by his modern biographers. (1) What is necessary are some basic principles of interpretation by which these facts can be woven into both psychological and spiritual portraits of his inner life. When it is a question of St. John's spiritual development, his writings, which depict the basic stages of the contemplative life, can serve as a general guide for arranging the few facts we possess, while for the psychological portrait Jung's work on psychological types is the most helpful norm. Psychological types represent the outer visibility of the process of individuation. In them this inner universal process is concretized in typical patterns. People of the same type, while maintaining their individuality, exhibit many common characteristics and have similar ways of thinking and behaving. Thus, if St. John's psychological type could be determined, the knowledge that exists about this type could help organize the facts we possess about his life, and lead to insights about the inner psychological states which gave rise to them. This is a risky business, especially when applied to a person in another time and culture. There is the danger of making an incorrect choice of type, or forcing the biographical material to fit preconceived notions. The only means of verifying the accuracy of the interpretation is its power to create a coherent psychological portrait that links the scattered facts together and sheds new light on them. What I would like to attempt, with these limitations in mind, is a psychological and spiritual portrait of St. John.

The estimation of a person's psychological type involves four interrelated judgments. The first three are decisions about whether the person is more extraverted or introverted, uses the function of sensation more or less than intuition, and uses the function of feeling more or less than thinking. The final judgment is often the most difficult, for it involves deciding which function is the most used or dominant, and as a consequence, that its alternative is the least developed, and which function acts as an aid or auxiliary to this dominant function, and as a consequence, its alternative is less developed. For example, someone whose predominant function is intuition would have as their least developed function sensation, and if they use their feeling function as the more developed aid to their intuition, their thinking function would be less developed.(2)

Three out of the four judgments about St. John's psychological type are relatively easy to make. St. John had a highly introverted personality, that is, his energy and attention were more focused on the world within rather than on the external world around him. His thinking function was more developed than his feeling function; (Jung considered thinking a way by which we come to a judgment of truth or falsity by the use of reason, and feeling a way of judgment by which we determine whether we like or dislike something) and finally, St. John's intuition, that is, the way he perceived the hidden implications or inner possibilities, was more developed than his power of sensation.

The fourth judgment is more difficult and more debatable. Is St. John an introverted intuition type with thinking as the auxiliary function, or is he an introverted thinking type with intuition as the auxiliary function? The evidence appears to favor the first interpretation, even though in practice these two types can often be difficult to distinguish. Not only is it important to see the evidence for St. John's type, but also to see his typological development, for that, as I have said, is an outer manifestation of the process of individuation.(3)

THE EARLY YEARS

Soon after John was born his father died from a long illness that had exhausted the material resources of the family. The poverty that had been kept at bay by the constant work of the mother and father as piecework weavers now became life-threatening. Apparently John's mother, Catalina, had nowhere to turn for help. Both the mother and father appear to have been orphans and, like St. Teresa, they might have been descendants from Jewish converts.(4) For some reason his father's family had vehemently opposed his marriage, yet after his death John's mother made a long and difficult journey to seek their help; she must not have had any other alternative. Most of these relatives rejected her pleas out of hand, though one of the uncles took the oldest son Francisco for a time. But this did not work out. Catalina, in her struggle to support her children, moved several times and ended up in Medina del Campo. Her middle son Luis died, and though Francisco began to work at the loom with her, she placed John in an orphanage. John was around nine years old at the time. It would be a mistake to view St. John's family life as one of unrelieved bleakness. His brother Francisco, 12 years older than John, appears as an engaging and congenial person who played an instrument, sang, and wandered through the streets of the town with his friends looking for diversion. His simple nature carried him along into some of their more destructive pranks, but his gentleness recoiled from these things and he began to lead a religious life, praying after work at the local churches and bringing homeless people back to their humble house. Francisco could well have been John's first example of joy amid trials and a serious dedication to the spiritual life. Yet Francisco's engaging simplicity precluded the drive and power of organization that would have allowed him to take over the family and better its economic condition. There may have been something more than sheer poverty that made John's mother place him in the orphanage. This could have been a growing realization that not only did John not have an aptitude for learning how to weave, but he had a lively intelligence that would benefit from schooling.

The introverted intuitive child can possess the pervasive feeling of not being at home in the world. By nature his intuitive gaze goes elsewhere, while his extraverted feeling and sensation functions which would help root him in the here-and-now remain undeveloped. He can possess an other-worldly nostalgia, and this conviction that his true homeland lies elsewhere can be reinforced by the misfortunes of his early years, which are seen as confirmations that this earthly life does, indeed, have not much to offer. Since St. John's earliest years were marked by genuine tragedies, dire poverty and the lack of any supportive extended family, it would not be surprising if these events resonated in his psychological type and later formed a background to the way he viewed the relationship between the mystical life and daily human existence.

There is one event from John's early years that allows us a glimpse at what might have been the beginning of his spiritual vocation. John was among a group of boys who were playing around a marshy pond on the outskirts of Fontiveros. They were throwing sticks into the water, and catching them as they popped up to the surface. When John reached to get his stick he lost his balance and fell into the pond and sank to the bottom, where his hands touched the mud. He momentarily came to the surface, and as he told his fellow Carmelites many years later, he saw within the pond area a beautiful lady who stretched out her hand to him, but he didn't want to give his hand to her because he didn't want to get her dirty. Fortunately, a laborer arrived who was carrying a board and drew him out.

Brenan gives another interpretation of this incident: "As he struggled in the mud and water he had seen a well-dressed lady on the bank whom he had taken to be the Virgin. He had stretched out his arms to her, but with the fists closed because his hands were too dirty to take hers."(5)

From a religious point of view St. John would be inclined to identify this beautiful lady with the Blessed Virgin, and given the traumatic circumstances of her appearance he would feel that he literally owed his life to her. His inward-turning consciousness now had a definite focal point, and perhaps his religious vocation began to crystallize. How could he accept the outstretched hand of the beautiful lady? What did it mean in terms of his own need to be worthy, and where would she lead him if he accepted?

This incident can be given a psychological interpretation as well. The beautiful lady appears when John has fallen from his everyday world into the dangers of another. She is within the circumference of the pond and invisible to all his companions. She is the bridge between consciousness and the unconscious, an anima figure which from a typological point of view embodies the feeling function which, in John, linked his ego consciousness of introverted intuition and thinking to the extraverted character of the unconscious manifested by extraverted feeling and sensation. An ambivalence often surrounds the figure of the anima. She was at once the way and the gate to an inner journey, and yet there is a reluctance to associate her in her spiritualized form with the less developed, cruder and materialistic aspects of the unconscious. John is unwilling to take her hand because his own is dirty. There is a cleavage between the inferior function of the extraverted sensation and this spiritualized anima. If we credit Brenan's account, the clenched fists symbolize the same reluctance. They can appear as a characteristic gesture of introverted intuition types, and are seen in an extreme form among schizophrenics in whom this type might well predominate.(6)

THE ORPHANAGE

If John's mother had actually perceived that her son's gifts did not embrace the weaver's loom, but were more intellectual in nature, then both of her judgments were vindicated by John's performance in the Colegio de la Doctrina. He turned out, in fact, to be an excellent student, but at the same time we are told that he was apprenticed in turn to a carpenter, tailor, wood carver and painter, but "he was soon returned as useless by all of them".(7)

The introverted intuition type often excels in academic work, while the inferior function of extraverted sensation can express itself in the kinds of failures that St. John experienced. This is not the result of a lack of manual dexterity or artistic ability in itself, but rather, the inability to focus the attention for any considerable length of time on the external physical work to be completed, especially if it is repetitive.

The tragedy of John's home life could have accentuated his already predominant introversion, his placement in this institutional setting would have only increased this process. He would not be the kind of boy who made friends readily, or could hold his own in a group where the more outspoken and aggressive personalities tend to dominate. His feelings would become submerged. The nuns found him suitable for taking care of the Chapel, but this is the kind of occupation that would tend to isolate him from his companions and the outside world, though it reinforced his religious inclinations.

HOSPITAL AND UNIVERSITY

John, as a teenager, entered the adult world by working in the Hospital of the Tumors which treated poor people in the last stages of syphilis. In the large halls filled with the sick and dying patients he saw another face of the misery of the world, yet strangely enough he was probably freer here and more expressive of his feelings, for throughout his life he showed a remarkable devotion to the sick. It was in their care that he would unbend and try to comfort them and obtain delicacies for them, and it is reasonable enough to assume that these feelings started with his work in the hospital. Perhaps the patients by the very fact and finality of their illnesses had been removed from the world, and John, who in his own way had no place in this world, saw them as in transit to the next. This made them his fellow travelers, and if he expressed himself about spiritual matters, the dying are often the most receptive audience.

The director of the hospital gave John permission to continue his studies at the recently formed college of the Jesuits. Here he received an excellent grounding in the classics and Spanish literature which equipped him not only for his studies for the priesthood, but was part of his poetic formation as well. The director, no doubt, was aware of St. John's academic abilities, and might have had one eye on the future even then. Here was a quiet and pious boy who was an excellent student and cared about the sick. What better choice for a chaplain for the hospital? This was an eminently reasonable suggestion, for it fit the outer facts about St. John, and it would have put him in a position to aid his mother and his brother who, by this time, was married and had children of his own.

The chaplaincy of the hospital was one logical move, and following in the footsteps of his young Jesuit professors would have been another, but John did the unexpected. To forestall any opposition he secretly went to the monastery of the Carmelites and took the habit. Whether this was the result of a slow inner development or was precipitated by some catalytic event is unknown. It is likely that St. John's devotion to the Blessed Virgin played a strong role in his selection of the Carmelites, for he wrote a poem in heroic verse about being received into the order of Our Lady. It is possible, as well, that the image of a life of prayer that he associated with the Order attracted him. Where can the fervor of beginners that St. John describes in his writings be found in his own life? The last months of his life at the hospital and the first of the novitiate are the most likely choices, but there is no evidence.

The new religious, now known as Juan of St. Mathias, after his novitiate was sent to the University of Salamanca. The Carmelite House of Studies there was small and consisted only of a handful of students who attended courses at home, as well as in the University proper. Fray Juan's interests were already centered on the mystical life, for he wrote a study about the authentic mystical tradition in the Church, which unfortunately was not preserved. When he was not attending lectures or studying or praying, he devoted himself to penance or fasting. He had no time for light conversations, and if he saw anyone breaking the rule he would reprimand them, as Brenan puts it, "with all the ardor and lack of tact of the neophyte". (8) The reaction of his fellow students, if not commendable, was understandable: "Let's be off - that devil is coming". He made only one friend. This is hardly a flattering portrait. St. John was an excellent student and a meticulous observer of the rule, both qualities that are often associated with his type, but he was also someone who had very definite ideas about his inner vocation. In some way, at some point, he had discovered his contemplative vocation, and having discovered it, was exerting all the energy of the powerful faculties of intuition and thinking that he was gifted with to pursue it. He had no time for anything else, and no inclination, and finally, no way of seeing the exterior effect of this single-mindedness. His selection of the Carmelites had been a selection based on spiritual motives rather than any realistic idea of how the Carmelites actually lived, and what their actual interest in the spiritual life was. It would not be conceivable to someone of St. John's temperament in this early phase of spiritual development that levity and a failure to observe every detail of the rule could co-exist with genuine spiritual aspirations. His conduct in reprimanding his fellow students is strikingly different from his habitual reserve and quiet, and the most probable answer for it lies in his understanding of the nature of religious life. While many things did not matter to St. John, one thing was of supreme importance: the will of God must be followed in all things great and small, and the rule was seen by him as a concrete embodiment of God's will for the present moment, and thus had an intrinsic connection with his search for holiness. Therefore, he felt compelled, despite his desire to efface himself, to speak out when it was a matter of his inner convictions. His fellow students, no doubt, took a less serious and weighty view of the matter. St. John's strict spiritual interpretation of the rule had a psychological dimension as well. The introverted intuition type often exhibits a meticulous and careful fulfillment of their obligations that can become tinged with scrupulosity. They are far removed from the everyday, normal ways of judging human situations. They can interpret the rule and the wishes of the people in authority in a much stricter fashion than others, and often stricter than the authorities themselves intended.

While St. John was in the novitiate where silence and devotion to the spiritual life predominates, he would have had less opportunity to see that the spiritual aspirations which motivated him to join the order were not shared in the same way by his fellow novices. In the small house of studies, however, with its relative relaxation of discipline, it became clear to him that he was among people who did not share his deepest aspirations. This conviction grew to the point where he decided to leave the order and seek a stricter and more solitary life among the Carthusians.

It is only his providential meeting with St. Teresa that prevented him from carrying out his plan. She convinced him that he could live out his spiritual quest within the new Reform, and thus remain in Our Lady's order. He could have an opportunity to whole-heartedly pursue the contemplative life under the banner, as it were, of the Blessed Virgin. St. John accepted, with only one condition, which highlights his intuitive nature; he did not want to wait long to begin.

ST. JOHN AND ST. TERESA

One indication that St. John, in his mid-twenties, by now had already passed through the first stage of the interior life and was an experienced contemplative was the relationship he had with St. Teresa. Teresa was 52 years old, and well advanced in the life of prayer, and actively engaged in establishing new monasteries. She was an impressive and attractive personality, yet John was never her disciple or protege. At the same time Teresa showed no emotional attraction to him. She admired his devotion to the spiritual life, and saw him as an excellent instrument for the Reform of both the friars and sisters, yet she did not warm to him.(9) From a psychological point of view this small, muddy-complexioned, deeply reserved man did not fit her image of the kind of man that would lead the reform movement to success. He never went out of his way to give in to her wishes. Further, they had disagreements about business matters concerning the founding of the houses, and St. John was not above doing things which he thought would be for her spiritual growth, even though he knew she would not like them. The most famous incident was when, knowing her desire for large Communion wafers, he gave her a small one. Brenan carefully draws out these temperamental differences and the difficulties that existed in their relationship, and while St. John and St. Teresa are in fundamental agreement about the nature of the mystical life, a simple reading of their works is enough to convince us that their basic personalities were highly diverse. What is the relationship, for example, between the visions and revelations that St. Teresa received and her own personality type? At the same time, the relationship between these two saints is a powerful argument for the way in which spiritual maturity overcame natural psychological inclinations. St. Teresa not only deeply admired St. John's devotion to the interior life, but she made use of him extensively in dealing with her sisters, taking advantage, on occasion, of his spiritual guidance for herself. When John was thrown in prison, hers was the only voice that was consistently and persistently raised in order to try to mobilize a rescue. In short, if she did not feel an emotional attraction to him, she did not let this cloud her spiritual perception.

St. John in these early years as an ordained priest behaved in exemplary fashion, yet the very intentness of his pursuit of his spiritual goal mingled with his temperamental introversion, produced the appearance of narrowness and reserve which St. Teresa obliquely remarked upon on several occasions. "God deliver us from people who are so spiritual that they want to turn everything into perfect contemplation", she once playfully wrote about him.(10)

If John at Salamanca, despite his life of prayer and penance, was chafing at the bit for an even more austere environment, then the first Carmelite house at Duruelo was perfectly suited to him. He shared it with just two or three people at the beginning, and he could wholeheartedly give himself over to the life of prayer. It was a decrepit building in which snow filtered through the boards and whose chief decorations were skulls and crucifixes. All was prayer and penance. Yet even here he engaged in some ministry. John never leaves the impression that working with and helping people bothered him in itself, but he had no interest in the social dimension of it. When, after celebrating Mass at a local parish, he was invited to dine with the parish priest, he would decline and sit on the edge of a field, munching his bread and cheese. Perhaps the very ramshackled nature of this house at

Duruelo appealed to John's nature. The accent was wholly
on the spiritual, and the inhabitants were more or less
oblivious to the material or sensation dimension. Soon his
mother and brother and brother's family came to stay with
him and handle many of the daily chores, which is a striking testimony to his affection for them and a counterbalance to an overly severe interpretation of his sayings
on detachment. This idyllic beginning was not destined to
last. Within eighteen months the reputation for holiness
of this little house had drawn so many recruits that they
were forced to move to larger quarters, and John was
caught up in helping to manage the growing population and
affairs of the Reform.

St. John's next assignment is significant for the light
it sheds on his own austerity and St. Teresa's view of it.
The novice-master of the Reform house at Pastrana had
taken to afflicting his new recruits with harsh and humili-
ating penances. This was an ever-present temptation in a
spiritual environment like Spain of those days, which
abounded with wandering holy people with visions and
bloody mortifications. To correct this situation, St. Teresa
sends St. John. As severe as St. John appears to us today,
he was seen by her as a moderating influence. It was not
in his nature to make penance an extravagant spectacle,
and he hid his own as best he could. He saw it only as
a tool to serve the ends of divine union.

From Pastrana he was appointed the rector of the
Carmelite house at the University of Alcala, but he was
not successful in this position:

"Although Juan's quiet, modest bearing created a favorable inpression, he lacked the dynamism and the gift for
making friends that were required for such an undertaking.
His whole bent was towards interior prayers and contemplation and although he could be firm and clear-sighted
where questions of principle or discipline were involved,
he was so averse to all practical affairs that he shrank
even from the office of prior."(11)

St. John's next position was much better suited to his
gifts. St. Teresa had been appointed prioress of her old
Convent of the Incarnation, and she selected St. John to
be one of its confessors. His time, therefore, was taken
up in a spiritual ministry to the one hundred and thirty
women. This was not a house of the Reform, but included
a wide range of factions, from sisters with a deep devo-

tion and attraction to the interior life to, no doubt, girls who by force of circumstances found themselves in the convent with no particular vocation to it. John was 30 years old when he took up this task, and this is his first extensive contact with women and the beginning of a ministry of spiritual direction to the sisters that was going to last throughout the rest of his life. If he seemed austere and forbidding from a distance, he made a much better impression the closer he was approached. While he could be terribly demanding when it was a question of the means best suited for a person to advance on the road to divine union, he was kind and gentle, especially to those who were afflicted. A proof of his success was the length of time St. Teresa kept him there. It stretched out over five and a half years, and was only ended by his kidnapping and imprisonment. We know very little about the effect of this stay on St. John himself. Certainly it was an opportunity to deepen his own spiritual life. Teresa reached her spiritual maturity during this time, and St. John had close contact with her. At the same time, a process of psychological maturation must have been going on as well. He could not spend hours every day listening to and advising these women without drawing on and developing his own feeling function, especially in its extraverted qualities. A move, however, to an increased use of extraverted feeling could also begin to constellate the question of the inferior function. Some of his first poetry and his habit of writing spiritual maxims, as well as a singular picture, can be dated from this time. Defying normal perspective, it shows a crucified Christ from above. It is an impressive forerunner of the artistic creations that were soon to emerge from the depth of St. John's soul in strange but beautiful images. St. John was moving towards a definitive transformation of both soul and psyche, and the very air around him was filled with the growing tension between the Reform movement and the rest of the Carmelite order.

PRISON

In early December of 1577, the Carmelite authorities broke into the little house next to the convent in Avila where St. John and his companion were staying, and carried them off. The Carmelite superiors had been growing increasingly frustrated and angry as they watched the Reform movement prosper and spread out and, in their minds, blatantly disregard their authority. They wasted no time in venting these feelings on the little upstart friar; as soon as they captured him they whipped him twice, and then secretly brought him to the Carmelite convent in Toledo. Soon word arrived of the escape of the other captured friar. The reaction of his own captors was swift. They threw him in a tiny cell that was lit only by a narrow aperture high on the wall, fed him on scraps of food, did not allow him to say Mass, and gave him no contact with the members of the house. Routinely they would drag him out before the whole community and make him kneel in their midst during mealtime, verbally abuse him, and then demand that each member strike him.

With John in their hands they gave way to vindictiveness. Not only was St. John intimately associated with the beginning of the Reform movement and close to St. Teresa whom they could not directly harm, but St. John's personality itself provoked them. He had a reputation from his earliest day in the order for austerity and perfection of life. At the same time, he possessed none of the extraverted masculinity that would have made him popular in the communities he lived in. He was the antithesis for any desire for authority and power, while he was maddeningly self-directed and motivated. Once he set a goal for himself he was not easily deflected. All these factors combined to make him the ideal victim of their projections. They saw him as a hypocrite who clothed in pious conduct his inward disobedience and self-willedness; they berated him as a "lima sorda", literally, a deaf lime. Any doubts they possessed about the legitimacy of their conduct towards him and the Reform they attempted to eradicate by brutalizing him and proving that he was really as bad as they made him out to be. Among men who rise to administrative power there is often a large percentage of extraverted thinking types with strongly developed sensation. St. John would represent for them the other side of their personalities, and be a convenient scapegoat upon which to project their own inferiorities and lack of development. As St. Teresa wrote to the King, "I would rather see him in the hands of the Moors."

What was the effect on John of such treatment? He was fresh from an atmosphere of quasi-veneration. The sisters and townspeople had held him in high regard, which had the effect of developing the extraverted dimension of his feeling function, and at least the posing of the difficult question of the inferior extraverted sensation. His imprisonment and his tormentors strike with an unerring evil instinct at this newly emerging dimension. John had a special preoccupation about being clean. He became covered with filth and vermin. The latrine bucket was left in his cell for days at a time. The light was so poor he had to attempt to read his breviary during the middle of the day, holding it up to the narrow slit in the wall. He was forbidden pen and paper until late in his imprisonment. He suffered from the cold of the Toledo winter that penetrated into his little stone room. His diet was so wretched he began to suffer from extreme diarrhea. He had no contact with his fellow friars except when he was brought out to be abused.

From a psychological point of view he was plunged into extreme introversion and cut off from the feeling and sensating dimensions, or rather, they became negative realities opposed to his conscious personality. It was as if a nightmare of the introverted intuition type had come true. This type loves freedom and movement, even though it is often expressed interiorly rather than in outer actions. The outer imprisonment would have been much more bearable if it were simply a care of exterior confinement. But St. John's torments went deeper. These were not strangers who were tormenting him, but people from his own religious family. He knew some of them personally, and the superior of the house had been his superior at the University of Salamanca. This superior hammered away at him, telling him that he was disobedient, for he was refusing to obey lawful commands. These tormentors actively played out the role of the negative aspects of his own extraverted feeling and sensation. John had always been concerned with an exact observance of the rule, motivated, as we have seen, by the belief that the rule embodied the will of God here and now. He began to wonder whether he was, indeed, disobedient.

His attacks of dysentery became so severe that he began to fear that his captors were poisoning him. He saw that it was a real possibility that he would die in prison. He began to worry that St. Teresa and his confreres in the Reform would think that he had given up and aban-

doned them. Cutting even deeper was the most painful
torment; what if he were wrong and really was disobedient
and obstinate? He would die in his sin and be eternally
damned.

The tension that had always existed in him between
conscious and unconscious, between the introverted intuition and the extraverted sensation, was now greatly increased. The unconscious began to manifest itself in opposition to the conscious viewpoint. The Calced authorities,
if they had wanted to poison him, could have done so
before without the effort of capturing him. Aside from St.
Teresa, there is little evidence of anyone in the Reform
devoting a great deal of energy and attention to his dis-
appearance. He was certainly not scandalizing them by
being captured and tormented. Further, St. John had a
carefully worked-out conscious position concerning under
whose authority his job as confessor to the convent in
Avila fell, and he had steadfastly maintained the legitimacy of this position in the face of all sorts of opposition
and even bribes. In short, his anxiety went beyond the
rational grounds for it. St. John was suffering from the
torments of scrupulosity that he would later describe in
the **Dark Night of the Soul.** These scrupulous ideas were
the result of the constellation of the unconscious whose
contents were seeking expression by fastening themselves
to some suitable conscious difficulty. The abusive superior
became associated with the inferior function, and St. John
began to see God distorted through these twisted emotions. Despite his conscious knowledge and experience to
the contrary, he conceives the possibility that God would
act in a petty and materialistic manner. God will not look
at the inner intent, but the outer material violation.

St. John was deep in his own night sea journey, having
been swallowed by the whale, as he put it. Working
through his physical and psychological sufferings was a
terrible spiritual agony that accentuated them. The beginning of a deeper, fuller union with God was assailing his
soul, and the pitiless light exposing the deep recesses of
human weakness and inclination to evil. This burning light
was transmuting John's weak human capacity for knowledge
and love to fit him for the heights of mystical union upon
which he would walk in the future. The description of
these spiritual torments and delights of this deeper life
in God are best to be found in his **Spiritual Canticle** and

Living Flame of Love.

While the torments predominated, he began to have moments of sublime mystical experiences as well:

"One evening, when he was in very low spirits, he heard a young man's voice singing a villancico or love song in the street outside...I am dying of love, dearest. What shall I do? - Die."(12)

An incident like this could have triggered the outpouring of his poetry, as well as his entrance to the heights of contemplation, for he wrote part of the poem the "Spiritual Canticle" in prison.

In the midst of his pain he was being transformed psychologically, as well as spiritually, a fact which will become clearer as we look at his life after Toledo. Within a few years after leaving prison most of his major poetry had been composed, and three of his four prose works initiated. He had reached a maturity out of which he could begin to definitively set down his ideas on the spiritual life. His poetry also played a pivotal role in uniting psychological and spiritual experience.

As summer with its stifling heat came to Toledo, John became weaker and weaker. He had been enduring his sufferings, and now he saw that further passivity would lead to his death. He could expect no mercy from the authorities, and there was no hint of imminent rescue. Slowly a series of events conspired to transform this passivity into action, yet action did not come easily or naturally to him. His nature was inclined to passivity, especially when it was a question of his own fate. He was assigned a new jailer who gave him more freedom, treated him with kindness, and provided him with a pen and paper. St. John started to write the poems that had been forming in his mind, and perhaps committing these poems to paper helped him see that this gift that had been given to him and that he had paid for with great pain could be a gift for others, but would never be of any use if he died in his miserable little cell.

The friars of the house who deliberately came close to St. John's cell to torment him with their conversations hit upon a strategy that undoubtedly had a great effect on him. They said, "Let's throw him in a well and no one will ever see him again." While this, no doubt, had an initial depressive effect upon him, for it confirmed his fears about their wishes for his death, it also might have helped stimulate his desire for escape. He could not help but remember the incident in his childhood in which he had fallen into the pool and would have drowned save for the appearance of the beautiful lady. As the summer wore on, he received interior impulses urging him to escape. His first biographer states that this came in the form of a vision of the Blessed Virgin. Will the beautiful lady again play a role in extracting him from an impossible situation? On the Vespers of the feast of the Assumption he was praying in his cell with his head to the ground, and his back to the door, when the superior unexpectedly entered and kicked him since he had not immediately arisen. The prior asked what he had been thinking about, and John told him how much he would like to celebrate Mass on the Feast of the Assumption. The prior brusquely refused, and left. John was going to have to celebrate the Feast of the Assumption in his own way. After making careful preparations, one night during the octave of the Feast, he forced his door, carefully crept from his cell and lowered himself on a rope he had made from his torn-up blanket, and dropped into a courtyard. He had acted and made a definitive move, but his problems were not automatically solved. He discovered that the courtyard belonged to a neighboring convent of nuns, and he was filled with despair because he was afraid of the scandal that would be given to people if he were discovered there in the morning. He almost gave up and called to his captors to come and get him, but somehow he overrode this scrupulosity and hypersensitivity and managed to scramble up one of the walls. Ragged and dirty, he wandered through the streets of Toledo "at an hour when the life of all cities is mysterious and strange."(13) The vegetable women saw him passing through the plaza as they arranged their wares for the market, and thinking he was coming back from some revel, shouted out dirty words to him. Finally, he found refuge for the remainder of the night in the vestibule of a house, emerged in the morning and made his way to the Discalced Convent of sisters, and they hid him within the cloistered walls.

Finally his ordeal was over, and he made his way back to his own world. Almost literally the first thing he did, despite his weakness and the aftereffects of his physical and psychological trials was to recite his poems to the sisters. We have a moving picture of him barely able to stand, softly uttering for the first time to other human beings the essence of his prison experience.

ANDALUSIA

Soon after his escape St. John made his way south to avoid the vengeance of the Calced authorities. He had been made prior of El Calvario deep in Andalusia. On the way to take up his new post he paused at the Discalced convent of Beas de Segura which was under the leadership of one of St. Teresa's most capable sisters, Ana de Jesús.

There was no transformation immediately evident in St. John in the first days of his new life in the south. His initial impression on Ana de Jesús was such that soon after she wrote St. Teresa lamenting the fact that she had no one to entrust the spiritual direction of the sisters to. St. Teresa immediately extolled the value of St. John for such a position. Soon John was making his way through the hills on periodic visits to the sisters. Perhaps the beauty and solitude of this countryside was slowly restoring his energy, and this energy, freer now because of his prison experience, began to express itself in a more overt fashion.

Without losing his reserved introverted nature, incidents began to appear that indicate he had become more expressive to the people around him and more enamored with the beauties of creation. He wrote another section of the poem "Spiritual Canticle", and the poem "On a Dark Night", which echoes his months of confinement and dramatic liberation. This poetic production overflowed in conferences to the sisters and in short maxims he gave to them, and finally the diagram of Mount Carmel and the way to ascend to its summit. Slowly these beginnings coalesced in the form of a commentary on his poem "On a Dark Night". Under the gentle interest and enthusiasm of the sisters, he also began to explain and comment on the "Spiritual Canticle". The sisters can be seen as visible, tangible, flesh-and-blood stimuli to St. John's extraverted feeling. Only now are the conditions ripe for St. John to express himself. He is among his sisters. The depth of this upwelling of feelings can be seen in the incident that occurred when he first arrived at Beas de Seguros from the north. The sisters were gathered in recreation, and one young girl began to sing of pains that are the garments of lovers. St. John was so overcome that he clung to the grill for an hour before he could recover himself.

It is during these months at El Calvario that we first begin to hear about St. John's love of nature as well. He would take the friars out into the fields and speak to them about the beauties of creation, and then they would disperse and find a spot by a stream or a rock to meditate. Often they would come back and find him absorbed to such a degree they had to tug on his habit to get his attention.

No doubt to his regret he was soon appointed the rector of a Carmelite House at Baeza, yet in contrast to his earlier appointment at the University of Alcala, he proved effective and popular, and much in demand as a spiritual director and for his scriptural and theological insights. But this activity, successful though it was, did not appeal to him. His own spiritual life was deepening and maturing, and calling him to solitude far away from the bustle of human affairs. He maintained his contact with the sisters at Beas and he would retire for days at a time to a little farm in the country that had been given to the friars. There he could give himself to prayer, and he would be inspired to speak to his companions about the wonders of the streams and stars. He maintained his feeling of being in exile that, as I have conjectured, was a constant element of his interior make-up. Now he projected it on the Andalusians whose more extraverted and vivacious nature was so at odds with his own, and he felt he had been exiled from his homeland of Castille. At the same time, never before in his life had he been surrounded by such a receptive audience. Slowly his reputation among the sisters and young friars had been growing. The young men who faced an appointment to his house with trepidation were greatly relieved to find how gentle he was at close quarters. Just as he had a passion for caring for the sick, he had an instinct for seeking out the troubled friar, speaking privately with him and staying with him until his mood lightened. John remained austere and given to penance, especially for himself. He did not let escape any opportunity to do the most menial jobs, and far from clinging to his role as prior, he employed it to give himself the freedom to humble himself before the whole community. Yet this is the same man who went out of his way to bring his brother Francisco south to live with him, and began to have some young men who acted as his assistants and follow him from house to house.

The Reform movement had finally won its autonomy, and this, together with its rapid expansion, led to a greater burden of administrative duties and the creation of a group of friars who preferred positions of leadership and the liveliness of the affairs of the order to the quiet and solitude of their cells. True to his type, St. John was against the expansion of the friars in the direction of more outside apostolic activity and foreign missions. He also thought it was inadvisable that men succeed themselves in office, for this would lead to their preoccupation with office-holding and winning elections to the detriment of the true interior goals of the order. As Brenan puts it, "to his contemporaries in the order he appeared negative and unimpressive because he displayed none of those active qualities which the rapid expansion of the Discalced seemed to require".(14) However, due to his role in the founding of the community and his spiritual reputation, he was constantly being elected to some position of authority.

John was appointed to the provincial council, and it was in this setting that he argued in favor of the contemplative character of the friars; so excited did he become, the chroniclers tell us, that he actually moved one or two steps from his place while he was speaking. Certainly this is a commentary both on his habitual reserve and the strength of his convictions on this matter. These convictions were rooted in his own spiritual perceptions, as well as his psychological nature, and as such he had ability to hold to them despite severe opposition. When the new leader of the Reform, Nicolas Doria, wanted to change and centralize the rule of the friars and transform the rule that St. Teresa had left to her sisters and drive out of the order his predecessor Gracián, St. John's voice was the only one raised in clear-cut, direct opposition. Even among his own friars, when it was a question of the observance of the rule, St. John could be severe in his discipline of any lapse.

John had come out of prison, not only into the beauty of Andalusia, but into what Jung called the second-half of life. He shouldered effectively a heavy load of leadership responsibility that went against his natural, conscious inclinations. Some of the narrowness had disappeared and he was much freer to speak of the things that mattered most to him. The old personality did not go away, but was broadened and deepened. St. John loved to find small, hidden places, but ones which had peep-holes looking out on wide vistas. Some of these views were from his tiny cell into the Chapel where the Blessed Sacrament was, but other views were out over the sweep of hills and fields to distant mountains. The physical beauty of the earth had become a symbol of the spiritual journey. During recreation he busied himself carving out what his contemporaries called "curious images", bringing to mind his famous picture from his time at Avila.

The possibility exists that St. John's personality was such that it helped provoke the harsh treatment that he received in Toledo. It is a certainty that in these later years his fearless denunciation of the policies of Doria brought upon him persecution and an attempt to oust him from the very order he had helped to found.

From a spiritual point of view St. John's increased ability to cope with positions of leadership went with a growing disinclination to do so. The more his inner life deepened, the more he found it difficult to deal with the affairs of men. He preferred to be among stones, he said, and became devoted to construction projects, perhaps another sign of psychological growth. In his later years he was not only the prior of the house in which he dwelt, but he became for a time the Vicar Provincial of Andalusia, a job that entailed a great deal of travelling in order to visit the houses of the Province. He also became one of the counselors to Doria. This was unfortunate because, as we have seen, he was no diplomat and never failed to speak his mind on essential matters. Doria, who could tolerate no overt opposition to his autocratic rule, launched a campaign to discredit John and drive him out of the order, or at least out of the country. He used as his tool in this work a friar who hated St. John for a reprimand he had once received, and who now went from monastery to convent trying to gather evidence to be used in stripping the habit from the order's co-founder. Finally, under these circumstances St. John had his wish that he would receive no office and was sent south as a preliminary step for a possible mission to Mexico. Here he fell sick, and died on Dec. 14, 1591.

THE POET

Both temperament and early environment influenced St. John's reserve and his teaching on detachment. The doctrine on self-abnegation, so evident in the **Ascent** and **Dark Night,** is much like John's personal appearance which put people off when they first made his acquaintance. His contemporaries saw a tiny, emaciated, dark-complexioned man in a tattered habit. How many could discern one of the greatest poets of Spain, and a future doctor of the Church?

We can read St. John today and become depressed as if we must exhibit a similar degree of mortification in order to progress in the spiritual life. Perhaps we have the wrong perspective. How much of St. John's reserve and insistence on detachment sprang precisely from the rich exuberance of his inner life? Was his doctrine on mortification more an effect of his inner experiences than a cause of them? Elements of type and environment were, no doubt, operative, but the power and beauty of these inner graces were stronger. They imposed on St. John the desire to hide himself, and with terrible clarity made him realize how foolish it would be to lose them for a lack of self-control.

If St. John's prose begins to weary us or make us heavy-hearted, we should turn to his poetry. This poetry, acclaimed as some of the finest in Spanish literature, has been scrutinized in order to elucidate St. John's dependence on earlier poetic forms, particularly the Song of Songs, Garcilaso de la Vega, and the popular tunes of his own time. And these dependences are both clear and extensive. Yet his freedom and mastery of his material fused it with his inner life and produced some strikingly original creations. St. John was not a poet as we normally conceive them. It is hard to imagine him being concerned about cultivating his poetic skills or the size of his output, nor would it have occurred to him to write a poem on a non-religious theme. This does not mean that he wrote in some kind of ecstatic trance which precluded the difficult effort of composition, but rather, that his poetry was intimately connected to his mystical experience, and at the service of it, as it were.

Another important aspect of St. John's poetic works is the unevenness of quality that they display; they do not all reach the same heights. His critics have recognized the preeminence of his "Spiritual Canticle" and "On a Dark Night", both written around the time of his imprisonment and escape. Even some of the poems written after this time, when John had advanced even further in the contemplative life and was a more experienced poet, failed to show the powerful lyric imagery of his finest work. For example, "Tras de un amoroso lance", while it pleases the intuition type with the imagery of flight and the mystic with its content, does not excite the critic. In the same way, "Entréme donde no supe", despite its close connection with contemplative experience, is more cerebral than the "Spiritual Canticle". This unevenness prompts Brenan, when commenting on the "Living Flame of Love", to ask, "Or had the conjunction of events that led to San Juan's brief poetic phase already passed?"(15)

Here we rejoin the theme of the interaction between individuation and contemplation. These prison poems express "a penetrating strangeness of tone that recalls, as very little poetry really does, the poignancy of dreams". (16) The actual prison experience, together with St. John's knowledge of Latin and Spanish poetry, and his meditation on the Scriptures, were the raw materials floating, as it were, in his inner subjectivity awaiting the moment when they would be of service in expressing this double inner transformation. This inner self was assailed by the graces of contemplative prayer and pierced by the sorrows, torments and longings that came to St. John as he lay abandoned in his cell. Both these powerful emotions and the dark fire of contemplation were stretching him to the breaking point. They were two tensions which reinforced each other. One was trying to overthrow the old man of sin, and the other, the old supremacy of the ego. Perhaps the song of the workman in the street outside his cell finally tipped the balance. From the lips of this most introverted of men bursts a song of astonishing vibrancy of feelings and sensual imagery. The very things of creation towards which St. John has manifested such reserve and restraint take on a numinous quality. He speaks of flowers, woods and meadows, and culminates in crying out, "Mi Amado, las montañas...My Beloved is the mountains, the wooded valleys lonely and sequestered, the strange and distant islands, the loud, resounding rivers, the loving breezes with their gentle whispers".(17)

From a psychological point of view St. John's poetry expresses a depth of feeling and sensation. This typological aspect is symbolized by the close connection that existed between the poetry and the Carmelite sisters. Virtually the first thing he did after escaping prison was to recite his poems to them. He dedicated the **Spiritual Canticle** to Ana de Jesús, and was transported into a deep state of emotion while listening to the singing of one of the sisters, as we have seen. It was a Carmelite nun, as well, that inspired him to complete the "Spiritual Canticle" by telling him that her prayer consisted in contemplating the beauty of God.

When St. John's poems burst forth, they traversed the unconscious and were shaped by its internal structure, its archetypal patterns, and clothed themselves in the images they found there. Mountains and rivers, la música callada, la soledad sonora, became the paradoxical symbols of the Beloved. The tensions were released, the spiritual met the things of sense, the integration of the psyche formed the living context for the union with God.

Much stranger than the fact that St. John's poetry is strongly marked by the qualities of the other side of his personality are the delicacy and quality of these poetic expressions. Both feelings and sensations show little of the lack of development that these functions in St. John must have possessed, nor do they evoke sexual overtones despite speaking in the language of lovers. Perhaps the reason for this is because we are not looking simply at an enantio-dramatic outburst of the unconscious side of the person-ality. We are faced with a genuine act of poetic creation which transcends the normal boundaries of expression from the unconscious. At the same time the mystical experi-ence, more powerful and deeply rooted than all else, transforms both the dimension of unconscious expression and the poetic act itself. Yet, despite the central role of the contemplative experience in St. John's poetry, it demanded an activation of the unconscious as the medium of passage through which it could direct itself towards consciousness and articulated expression, and find the rich imagery while transforming it that gives St. John's best poems such a deeply human as well as spiritual character. Without the transformation of the psyche that had its critical turning point in Toledo, St. John's poetry would never have reached the heights it did.

MAJOR PROSE WORKS

A knowledge of St. John's poetry is perhaps the best safe-guard to avoid being put off completely when starting to read his prose commentaries. The reactions to picking up the **Ascent of Mount Carmel** or the **Dark Night** range from incomprehension to depression tinged with boredom, as St. John appears to engage in endless divisions and subdivisions, and a merciless rooting out of human desires. Our reaction can be, "This may well be fine for people in cloisters who are receiving mystical graces, but does it really speak to us today?" A knowledge of his poetry can prevent us from too quickly labeling St. John as negative and privative and turning away. Yet it puts us in a dilemma. What kind of man could pen both the verses of the "Spiritual Canticle" and the commentary on the **Ascent** and **Dark Night**? Why does St. John adopt such a rigorous scholastic prose when commenting on his poems? The key to the resolution of this paradox lies in the very nature of his poetry as a production both of the mystical experiences he underwent, and the depth of his own unconscious. Neither mystical experience nor those roots of the unconscious in which poetic intuitions are born, are the realm of clear ideas and distinctions. When St. John recited his poems to his sisters in the Order of Mount Carmel, he knew he was uttering "mystical sayings born out of love", and while he had sometimes sought for the words in which to express this love, at other times he felt the words were given to him, and even with a sense of inspiration he was deeply and painfully aware of how inadequate any explanation would be in relationship to the actual experience. When the sisters at Beas heard the "Spiritual Canticle" they wanted an explanation of it, reasoning, naturally enough from a commonsense point of view, that the author could explain the magical symbols in it. In essence, the reason why St. John had difficulty in writing commentaries on his poetry was because in a very real sense he did not know what they meant. There was no equivalent conceptual explanation at his fingertips for the kinds of experiences he had undergone, even though some sort of strange knowledge was associated with them. He says in the Prologue to the **Spiritual Canticle**:

"Who can describe the understanding He gives to loving souls in whom He dwells? And who can express the experience He imparts to them? Who, finally, can explain the desires He gives them? Certainly, no one can! Not even they who receive these communications. As a result these persons let something of their experiences overflow in figures and similes, and from the abundance of their spirit pour out secrets and mysteries rather than rational explanations."(18)

He finds in this method of proceding a close analogy with the Song of Songs and the rest of Scripture, "where the Holy Spirit, unable to express the fulness of His meaning in ordinary words, utters mysteries in strange figures and likenesses." This brings us closer to understanding something of St. John's use of Scripture. He was attracted to some of its "strange figures and likenesses" since they seemed to him to be authentic expressions of the hidden mysteries, and thus a kind of guarantee to his own groping to express his mystical experience. Thus, St. John had a sense of how his commentaries were bound to fall short and appear inadequate. He is going to explain his verses only in a general way and not exclude other possible interpretations, for the possibility of other interpretations resides in the disparity between the richness of the symbols and the thinness of the conceptual statements.

From a psychological point of view we are face-to-face with the birth of multi-faceted archetypal symbols that are susceptible to a number of different interpretations, all equally valid and referring to different levels of being enfolded in the one symbol.

The very nature of this kind of poetic creation allows us to understand some of the puzzling facts surrounding St. John's literary career. St. John, according to our hypothesis, was an introverted intuition type who was transfixed, as it were, by the splendor and beauty of his inner experiences. While he was a clear and concise thinker, he had no gift of rhetoric like so many preachers of his day. When he started out to comment on the poem "On a Dark Night", he began in all good faith to attempt to treat of it verse by verse. But his commentary was a production of his consciousness. His sense of order and logic soon led him into many by-ways and supplementary explanations, and what began to emerge was something quite different from his original intention. He loses sight of the poem and follows the thread of the logical argument, and then pursues that with great rigor. In the **Spiritual Canticle** he again is attempting a commentary on the poem, but even when he forces himself to produce explanations of the words, they fall flat. The commentary on the **Ascent** rolls on and on with its own momentum, and then it is as if suddenly St. John awoke to the fact that things are not going like he originally desired, and he was faced with a seemingly insuperable task to complete the logical explanation, and like many intuition types, he breaks off in sight of the goal. The inadequacy of his explanation inspired him to begin again and comment anew on the "On a Dark Night", giving us the treatise the **Dark Night**, but here, again, his plans go awry. The inadequacy of conceptual expression for symbolic realities could also shed light on the question of St. John making more than one redaction of some of his works.

If St. John, conceptually speaking, had to grope to express the meaning of his poems, then we can understand some of the difficulties in reading his prose. He seemed to be constantly coming back to the same points and approaching them from different directions and hedging them about with parentheses and circumlocutions. He acted like a man who had something to say and can't really come out straight and say it. If his prose begins to close in on us and his divisions weary us and his expressions of abnegation depress us, we should return to his poems in order to renew our sense of the beauty and freedom that must have existed in the contemplative experiences themselves. St. John recognized that there were more meanings concealed in these poems than he could ever utter. Each of us as a unique individual will have a distinctive way of understanding this poetry, and through it interpreting his prose, for each of us is called in a unique way to the same experiences that gave birth to both. If we understand the nature of St. John's prose, we can be more tolerant when we hit upon its limits, and in a better frame of mind to appreciate the superlative, positive qualities it possesses with its incisive analyses and masterful descriptions.

And if finally, as we have been maintaining, St. John's poetry is the product both of his mystical experiences and the concomitant process of individuation, then his prose expositions in their own way will show these same two inner transformations, which brings us to the task of the next chapter.

CHAPTER 7

PSYCHIC ENERGY AND CONTEMPLATION

If Jung's typology represents one aspect of the process of individuation, his theory of compensation and psychic energy describes another, and is a valuable way in which to explore the psychological dimension of St. John's teaching on the passage to contemplation.

PSYCHIC ENERGY

Jung summarized his ideas on psychic compensation in a long but important passage in **Psychological Types:**

"Psychologists often compare consciousness to the eye: we speak of a visual field and a focal point of consciousness. The nature of consciousness is aptly characterized by this simile: only a limited number of contents can be held in the conscious field at the same time, and of these only a few can attain the highest grade of consciousness. The activity of consciousness is **selective.** Selection demands **direction.** But direction requires the **exclusion of everything irrelevant.** This is bound to make the conscious orientation one-sided. The contents that are excluded and inhibited by the chosen direction sink into the unconscious, where they form a counter-weight to the conscious orientation. The strengthening of this counterposition keeps pace with the increase of conscious one-sidedness until finally a noticeable tension is produced. This tension inhibits the activity of consciousness to a certain extent, and though at first the inhibition can be broken down by increased conscious effort, in the end the tension becomes so acute that the repressed unconscious contents break through in the form of dreams and spontaneous images. The more one-sided the conscious attitude, the more antagonistic are the contents arising from the unconscious, so that we may

speak of a real opposition between the two. In this case
the compensation appears in the form of a counter-function, but this case is extreme. As a rule, the unconscious
compensation does not run counter to consciousness, but
is rather a balancing or supplementing of the conscious
orientation."(1)

Underlying this psychological principle of compensation
is a view of the psyche in terms of psychic energy. The
psyche is conceived as a bipolar system which embraces
a series of pairs of opposites: conscious and unconscious,
thinking and feeling, introversion and extraversion, spirit
and matter, etc. These opposites create a tension which
is the source of psychic energy. Jung surmised that the
psyche could be conceived as a relatively closed system
in which basic laws of energy following the model of
physical energy hold sway. The chief of these laws is the
principle of equivalence:

"The principle of equivalence states that for a given
quantity of energy expended or consumed in bringing about
a certain condition, an equal quantity of the same or
another form of energy will appear elsewhere."(2)

In this connection psychic energy is not intrinsically one
particular kind of energy; it is not qualitative, but quantitative. Each psychic content has a certain amount of
energy which can increase or decrease. How much psychic
energy a particular content has is a value judgment. We
like something more or less, or feel something is better
for us than something else. In consciousness we are aware
of these transformations of energy. We lose interest in one
thing and begin to value something else more highly. But
how is it possible to estimate the energetic values of
unconscious contents? Here "the constellating power of the
nuclear element corresponds to its value intensity, i.e., to
its energy."(3) This constellating or attractive power can
be measured in various ways. Early in his career, for
example, Jung carried out a series of word association
experiments in which he physically measured the hesitations that surrounded particular words. These hesitations
were caused by the energy that had accumulated around
various unconscious contents.

When there is an adequate adaptation to reality, the
flow of psychic energy is smooth and the opposites contained in the psyche are united in working towards the
same goal, and this produces a feeling of vitality and a

sense of balance. However, under the pressure of new demands, the opposites tend to work in different directions, the flow of energy is impeded, often one of the opposing forces is repressed and an unresolved tension grows in the psyche. In St. John's writings there exist descriptions that exemplify Jung's principle of equivalence and the dynamics of psychic energy.

OUTBURSTS OF SENSE

In his discussion of the faults of beginners in the first book of the **Dark Night** he speaks about spiritual lust:

"It happens frequently that in one's very spiritual exercises, without one's being able to avoid it, impure movements will be experienced in the sensory part of the soul, and even sometimes when the spirit is deep in prayer or when receiving the sacrament of Penance or of the Eucharist."(4)

St. John found three reasons for these feelings, and all of them are "outside one's power"(5). The first cause is due to the fact that the sensual and spiritual parts of man form one personality, and "each one usually shares according to its mode in what the other receives"(6). Thus, when the spirit experiences satisfaction in God, the senses experience gratification.

The second cause is the devil who "excites these feelings while souls are at prayer, instead of when they are engaged in other works, so that they might abandon prayer"(7). The third cause of these impure feelings is the fear the person has of them. "Something that they see or say or think brings them to their mind, and this makes them afraid, so that they suffer from them through no fault of their own"(8).

With this third reason St. John comes close to framing a psychological explanation. He is also aware of how difficult this state of impure thoughts can be to melancholics: "The devil, they think, definitely has access to them without their having the freedom to prevent it...If these impure thoughts and feelings arise from melancholia, a person is not ordinarily freed from them until he is cured of that humor, unless the dark night close in upon the soul and deprives it successively of all things"(9). He also suggests that some people are more susceptible to these movements than others, for their natures are "delicate and tender, their humors and blood are stirred up by any change"(10).

St. John's explanations can be complemented by viewing these same phenomena according to Jung's hypothesis on psychic energy. The sensory movements happen frequently "in one's very spiritual exercises and in the reception of the Eucharist"(11). This timing is significant, and St. John emphasizes it in his descriptions: "...For they think these feelings come while they are engaged in prayer rather than at any other time. And this is true..."(12)

Consciousness forces its attention to spiritual things, and this process of selection necessarily tends to force the consideration of sensible things into the unconscious. If this process is continued for any length of time, as it is in someone who habitually cultivates a life of prayer, it is easy for these neglected contents to begin to build a counter-force to consciousness. Precisely when the consciousness is reaching towards the most pure spirituality, it is furthest removed from that which is sensual, and therefore, the tension between the two opposites is greatest, and from an energetic point of view, the energy that the neglected contents have is highest. Therefore, at the very moment of spiritual seeking the devil "succeeds in portraying to them very vividly things that are most foul and impure"(13).

What energy the sensual contents lose in consciousness by neglect, they pick up in the unconscious. This means that the sensual content in the unconscious should increase in constellating power because its energy charge is higher. This constellation is not only manifested by the emergence of the impure contents, which we have just seen, but also by the emotional affects connected with these contents which now emerge. The constellated content tends to gather around it a growing number of associative satellites held in its orbit by its new energetic intensity. The result is "that those who are affected by this dare not even look at anything or meditate upon anything because they immediately encounter this temptation"(14). This, as I have said, is a result of the high energy level of the neglected content which can immediately capture and transform innocent objects.

"And upon those who are inclined to melancholy this acts with such effect that they become greatly to be pitied since they are suffering so sadly; for this trial reaches such a point in certain persons, when they have this evil humour, that they believe it to be clear that the devil is ever present with them and that they have no power to prevent this."(15)

Melancholy in this context can be understood as a lack of energy available to consciousness for the pursuit of its activities; therefore, this class of person would fall prey more easily to the energized contents in the unconscious. Melancholy remains a generic classification which does not indicate the origins of this lack of conscious libido. The ultimate phase of opposition, the continual presence of the devil, can be equated with the emergence of the counter-function. The unconscious is in open opposition to the conscious attitude and gives it no peace. Consciousness is on the defensive, and its very fear and exertions to free itself from these temptations only render them more intensive, for it increases their energy, and so St. John very aptly describes the fear these people have as one of the sources for these impure motions.

TEMPTATIONS AND CONTEMPLATION

It is possible to view the beginning of contemplation from the energetic standpoint as well. The prayer of beginners that was summed up under the headings of medi-tation and sensible spirituality is characterized by a cer-tain harmony. The beginner has turned from the world which denied outlet to his spiritual aspiration and has found a new situation in which he experiences a vital feel-ing of satisfaction by attaining a viewpoint that comprises both God and the things of sense. This conversion stage is not simply the denial of the world and an embracing of the spiritual; in a very real way it is a harmony of the spiritual and sensible where God feels close and the spiri-tual world yields sensible satisfaction. The beginner experi-ences sensible delights in the pursuit of his spiritual goals. The tension between God and the world has been overcome and the two opposites, both sense and spirit, are working together.

Unfortunately, as pleasant as this state is, it cannot last. St. John is adamant in asserting that since God tran-scends what can be attained by any of the human facul-ties, then spiritual progress demands leaving the knowledge that can come through these faculties and proceding by faith. The glorious wholeness that was experienced in the sensible analogate of mystical experience begins to fade. Both St. John and St. Teresa describe this transformation in terms of water imagery, which also played a role in Jung's description of psychic energy.

St. John likens the period of sensible spirituality to the flowing of sweet spiritual water which the beginner tastes "wheresoever and for as long as they desire"(16). However, there are essential limitations to how much water can come through the natural faculties which are conduits and pipes that bring it from afar. Contemplation, on the other hand, remedies this situation by making the water spring up in the very midst of the soul without the need of the efforts of meditation.

The transition, though, can be very difficult and traumatic:

"When they are going about these spiritual exercises with the greatest delight and pleasure, and when they believe that the sun of Divine favour is shining most brightly upon them, God turns all this light of theirs into darkness, and shuts against them the door and the source of the sweet spiritual water which they were tasting in God whensoever and for as long as they desired."(17)

It is as though the maximum water is being transported by the system of meditation, and when even greater demands are put upon it, it fails. If it did not fail, all the energy and effort that is bound up with it would not be released and made available in preparing the soul for what is to come, and the beginner would not realize his radical inability in achieving contemplation. Adaptation has broken down and a creative tension arises, hopefully out of which a new balance will come. This tension marks the whole period of the night of sense which is the period of initiation into contemplation.

In the night of sense, instead of being fed, the natural faculties must be mortified. From an energetic point of view the night of sense is the passification of the sensible man by aridity. This aridity and privation which empties the natural faculties is the hidden onslaught of contemplation, which is a different and higher light which blinds the soul to its ordinary ways of praying. Its purpose is to strip it of its limitations that come to it in virtue of its senses. The soul "loses the strength of its passion and concupisence and it becomes sterile because it no longer

consults its likings...the desires of the soul are dried up."
(18) This phenomenon St. John describes in his commentary
on the verse "my house being now at rest". "The four
passions of the soul - which are joy, grief, hope and fear
- are calmed through continual mortification"(19); the night
of sense quenches natural energy and concupiscence.

But if the natural energy which works through consciousness is quenched, what happens to it? In accordance
with the principle of equivalence, we should expect to see
it emerging elsewhere. In actual fact, there is extensive
phenomena which surrounds the night of sense and the
transition to contemplation which were carefully described
by St. John, which can be attributed to this reappearance
of energy in different forms.

For example, in the **Living Flame** St. John describes
how:

"with hardly any trouble, the devil works the greatest
injuries, causing the soul to lose great riches, and dragging
it forth like a fish, with the tiniest bait, from the depths
of the pure waters of the spirit, where it had no support
or foothold but was engulfed and immersed in God."(20)

But how is it that the smallest bait can have such an
attraction for the soul precisely when it is beginning to
enjoy this higher spiritual experience?

In the **Ascent of Mount Carmel** John is describing "the
fight against the beast of the Apocalypse and its seven
heads, which are in opposition to these seven degrees of
love"(21). It is unfortunate that those who have conquered
the first heads of the beast and are "passing out of the
state of meditation" should find themselves conquered by
this beast "at the moment of their entrance into purity
of spirit"(22). And even the attraction to sense objects
which they had overcome early in the struggle is revived.
Why is it that the beast arises precisely at this moment
and even his first head, attachment to sense, comes to
life?

St. John's stress on the role of the devil underlines the
autonomous quality of these temptations. His explanation,
however, could not at that time go another step and
recognize the compensatory relationship between the spiritual attitude of consciousness and the movements of sensuality in the unconscious. A distinct pattern is now
emerging. Precisely at the moment when the soul is to
pass over into a more spiritual way, it is attacked by a

resurgence of sense; the heads of the dragon come alive again. The tiny bait of sense becomes irresistible, and foul and impure images can flood the mind. There are other phenomena which round out this picture and give us another view of the devil at work.

"For the evil one takes his stand, with great cunning, on the road which leads from sense to spirit, deceiving and luring the soul by means of sense, and giving it sensual things...And if perchance any soul enters into recollection, he labours to bring about its ruin by means of horrors, fears or pains of the body, or by outward sounds and noises, causing it to be distracted by sense, in order to bring it out and distract it from the interior spirit, until he can do no more and so leaves it."(23)

As the beginner nears contemplation, the things of sense become more attractive, and if he eludes these sirens and enters into recollection, all hell breaks loose and attempts to drag him out. It is significant that these horrors, fears, pains and noises are meant to distract it by means of sense. Here again it is a case of high spirituality being accompanied by low sensuality.

Finally, if the person is being called by God to a high degree of spirituality, he or she can be subjected to the most extreme temptations of all, a kind of final outburst of sensuality.

"For to some the angel of Satan presents himself - namely, the spirit of fornication - that he may buffet their senses with abominable and violent temptations, and trouble their spirits with vile considerations and representations which are most visible to the imagination, which things at times are a greater affliction to them than death."(24)

The form of this first temptation parallels St. John's discussion of the sin of spiritual lust. Acute purity of spiritual intent is matched by gross sensuality.

"At other times in this night there is added to these things the spirit of blasphemy, which roams abroad, setting in the path of all the conceptions and thoughts of the soul intolerable blasphemies. These it sometimes suggests to the imagination with such violence that the soul almost utters them, which is a grave torment to it."(25)

Here, again, the structure of this phenomenon is similar to the first temptation; the dwelling of consciousness on the infinite purity and goodness of God again has the impact of calling into being a countermovement which attempts to balance it.

"At other times another abominable spirit, which Isaias calls **Spiritus vertiginis**, is allowed to molest them not in order that they may fall, but that it may try them. This spirit darkens their senses in such a way that it fills them with numerous scruples and perplexities, so confusing that, as they judge, they can never, by any means, be satisfied concerning them, neither can they find any help for their judgment in counsel or thought."(26)

The introduction of temptations to scrupulosity recalls St. John's trials in prison and presents a new facet in the phenomena that accompany the transition to contemplation. The root of scrupulosity lies in the inability to make a judgment about the value of certain conscious contents, whether they be good, bad or indifferent. The sufferers of this torment, as St. John says, cannot find any help for their judgment in counsel or thought, which is an indication that the problem does not lie in the realm of conscious decision. Therefore, we should look to the unconscious and its highly energized contents which are attempting to manifest themselves by way of scrupulosity. Those neglected contents, since they have no ordinary avenues of expression, emerge by way of various states of guilt and anxiety, and fasten themselves to conscious contents. The affect which then accompanies these conscious contents is out of proportion to the actual contents themselves, though in many cases these states of affect are selective in their choice of what they fasten onto. Scrupulous people are often scrupulous about a particular kind of thing, and this class of contents is related to the repressed and unassimilated contents in the unconscious.

INFLATION AND DEFLATION

In all these temptations the imagination plays a vital role. It is the imagination that holds up the images from the senses to the transforming forces from the unconscious. It becomes the arena in which conscious and unconscious struggle to achieve a new relationship.

The beginner is puffed up by his spiritual experiences. He attributes them to himself. From the psychological point of view, this is a state of inflation where the ego attributes to itself realities that are not its own proper possessions. St. John's description of the imperfection of beginners is a whole catalogue of these inflationary phenomena.(27) These beginners develop a vain desire to speak of spiritual things, to instruct rather than be instructed, to condemn others. They want no one except themselves to appear holy, and even make manifestations of this holiness in outward signs. They want their spiritual director to think good of them and to do what they want. They are not content with the spirit God gives them, and are distressed when their consolation diminishes. They measure the things of the spirit by their own sensible satisfactions. They want to be praised, and are envious of those who seem to be making progress.

The inflation of the beginners is quenched by the trials and temptations they undergo. The balance of energy has shifted to the unconscious. They are subjected to autonomous powers that buffet them and threaten to overwhelm them. Deflation follows inflation.

WHOLENESS AND HOLINESS

There are two important questions that arise from exploring the dynamics of psychic energy in St. John's descriptions of the trials of the spiritual life. The first is a practical one. How should a person act in this state? Here, in the past, the priest and the psychologist had different perspectives. If the priest viewed these temptations simply as such, that is, as the work of the devil or the weakness of the flesh, then he would logically advise the person to resist and fight these temptations as evil. The psychologist, for his part, because he is aware that there can be a direct relationship between the person's spiritual aspirations and these outbursts of sensuality, and that the two from a psychological point of view are elements that go to make up the whole psyche, realizes that these unpleasant contents cannot simply be repressed. For him this evil is as real as the good, and is a constitutive part, with the good aspirations, of the human psyche. We have returned, then, on the practical plane, to the epistemological problems that came up in Chapter Two.

There are, then, two kinds of interacting ethical systems that run through all these considerations and should be clarified further. The first is the psychological ethic where the accent is on the striving for human wholeness;

consciousness must be suitably enlarged and the shadow or regressive and unpleasant aspects of the personality integrated. Without the undertaking of this painful effort not only will man not reach his full psychic stature, but he will become a social menace who finds his own worst weaknesses in others. Within this system the ethical goal is to be found in finding the midpoint of the total personality around which consciousness and the unconscious will balance. Overemphasis of either dimension of the personality will be a psychological ill that must be redressed. The law of ethical compensation is paramount because without its recognition, ethical efforts become one-sided and produce the effect opposite to what was originally intended. The underlying foundation of ethical compensation is a view of the full extent of the psyche which extends beyond consciousness.

Traditional morality, on the other hand, stands in contrast to this psychological ethic, for it is concerned primarily with conscious intent and free choice; and it is holiness that is sought above all else rather than wholeness; the will of man must be in accord with the will of God. Each of these systems has its own purpose and validity, but since they are operative within the same concrete individual they can appear at odds with each other because both often make use of the same material and vocabulary, but for contrasting ends. These differences will appear again in the context of spiritual direction, as they already have in relationship to the doctrine of the Quietists.

CONTEMPLATION AND INDIVIDUATION

James Kirsch, a noted Jungian analyst, once asked Jung whether St. John's dark night of the soul was a process of individuation, and he replied, "John of the Cross' "Dark Night of the Soul" has nothing to do with this. Rather, integration is a conscious confrontation, a dialectical process..."(28) This brings us to the second question. Though there is a substratum of psychic dynamics underlying St. John's descriptions of the passage to contemplation, it would be precipitous to conclude either contemplation represents some kind of individuation or it is the result of the resolution of these tensions of psychic energy. At the same time it would be a valuable undertaking if the contemplative life would be examined from

the point of view of Jung's psychology. In this way a
description that would be tangential to that of the theologians could be developed which would highlight the transformations of psychic energy that take place on this inner
spiritual journey. The theologian must assert the transcen-
dent nature of contemplation in itself, but he can no
longer do this without any reference to the nature of the
psyche in which this contemplation is experienced. If contemplation demands a thoroughgoing program of mortification and a definite attitude of passivity when it is present, and thus could occasion the outbursts of sensuality
that St. John describes, then it is crucial to arrive at a
solution to these difficulties. The struggling contemplative
needs both spiritual and psychological guidance. St. John
provides the spiritual advice by pointing out the danger
of ignoring this dawning contemplation because it is not
as palpable as the natural working of the faculties. But
from a psychological point of view the degree of psychic
tension will be a result not only of the depth of the contemplative gift, as St. John implies in discussing the three
temptations of those called to the heights of contemplation, but it will also be a function of the person's own
degree of psychological integration. Any psychic weakness
or lack of integration will accentuate the tensions occasioned by the impact of contemplation on the psyche. If
a program of individuation could be tailored for the contemplative that would still allow him to maintain the contemplative goal as his central focus, it would, no doubt,
ameliorate the trials that he must undergo. St. John,
discussing spiritual lust, says: "If these impure thoughts and
feelings arise from melancholia, a person is not ordinarily
freed from them until he is cured of that humor, unless
the dark night flows in upon the soul and deprives it
successively of all things."(29)

As St. John indicates, there can be both a psychological as well as a spiritual approach to the same question,
and in the darkness of his cell in Toledo he underwent a
process that transformed him both spiritually and psychologically. In summary, we can trace the interaction of contemplation and individuation in St. John's life, poetry and
doctrine about the beginning of mystical experience. Next
this dual perspective will be focused on these questions
about the life of prayer.

CHAPTER 8

BEGINNERS AND CONTEMPLATIVES

Hopefully the preceding chapters have begun to outline an instrument with which we can examine some of the problems of the life of prayer today. This instrument consists of both Jung and St. John, individuation and the journey to contemplation. In this chapter, after a few remarks on spiritual direction, I will examine the state of beginners and contemplatives, and in the next that of those who are neither beginners or contemplatives but live in the strange land inbetween.

SPIRITUAL DIRECTION

Spiritual direction here means explicit guidance in how to progress in the life of prayer, and today it is difficult to talk about a viable science of spiritual direction actually existing. Among clergy and members of religious communities the possibility still exists of finding a spiritual director, though the quality of this direction will vary greatly. But in regards to the vast majority of Churchgoing people, there is simply no spiritual direction either offered or sought.

Whatever may have been the state of development of spiritual direction in past ages, the renewal of it today is more than a matter of reviving the past. Its intimate nature is linked not only to an understanding of prayer itself, but the psychology of the people who are attempting to pray. On the practical plane, the most promising avenue of development appears to be under the guidance of St. John with the help of Jung's psychology.

SPECULATIVE AND PRACTICAL SCIENCE

St. John did not take a speculative approach in writing about the life of prayer. He was not interested in knowing things in themselves without any reference to the goals to be attained. He left us no treatises on dogmatic or moral theology, but he embraced aspects of both, and employed them in what Maritain called a "practically practical science".(1) St. John's science of spiritual direction was not simply a part of moral theology which views in a speculative way what ought to be done, but rather, it occupied a position midway between moral theology and the choices of the unique individual which will never be repeated and never become the object of science. The very formulation of the concepts St. John used and the intimate texture of his thought were shaped by his goal of leading a person to union with God. No matter how pregnant with ontological values his writings are, they are geared to this specific end. They fill the gap between the more general exhortations of moral theology and the actual concrete decisions of the individual.

But St. John's practical science of prayer needs to be complemented by an equally practical psychological science. Spiritual directors in the past could draw on a philosophical psychology that talks about human nature in general, and some rules of thumb imperfectly abstracted from individual experience, but they had no practically practical science, no science standing in the middle and geared for action, and this lack is one of the chief reasons for the decline of spiritual direction.

We have only to look at Jung's psychology, especially his typology, to be struck at how well it fills this gap. Typology explores those traits which stand between the universal characteristics common to us all and those that are uniquely our own. If employed as a visible manifestation of the whole process of individuation, it could provide the missing psychological instrument for the renewal of spiritual direction. It opens the possibility of beginning to explore the characteristic ways in which people experience the spiritual life, and this kind of knowledge, in its turn, can shed light on what can be called the typical problems of religious communities in which the mixture of various psychological types lead to misunderstandings and conflicts.

TYPE AND COMMUNITY

The early history of the Discalced Carmelites provides us with an example of difficulties of this sort. The early days of the Reform at Duruelo with their poverty and tiny community delighted St. John, but such a daring and literal interpretation of the Gospel has always been attractive. Crowds of recruits ranging from young students to old hermits flocked to join the new Reform. They naturally possessed a wide range of psychological types and spiritual inclinations, and this indiscriminate recruitment bore the seeds of later dissention. Parties arose both for and against the missions, and for and against active apostolic work and preaching. St. John's voice was sometimes lost amidst the chorus of more active, extraverted personalities whose capacity and talent for organization made them thirst to get their hands on the reins of government and exercise power. The tension that grew up between St. John and Doria is by no means unique. We have only to look at the problems between St. Francis of Assisi and Brother Elias, or between the early hermits and a St. Basil to realize that there are archetypal patterns that constantly reappear in the history of religious communities.

These same kinds of human differences show themselves within the daily life of religious communities. In traditional communities there were regulations that covered all the details of ordinary existence. They delineated the time that could be given to sleep, the kinds and quantities of food, the type and length of prayers, the variety of penances that were permissible. Unfortunately, even though such laws were often framed with the idea in mind that they in some way embodied the will of God, they did not and could not eliminate legitimate human differences. Is it possible to apply such uniform laws to different types without this becoming a form of discrimination?

The importance of these differences goes beyond the give-and-take of daily community life, and has an effect on the pursuit of holiness of the individual members. There are, no doubt, distinctive modalities of holiness that rest on typological foundations, and they give rise to different paths of development. Individual aptitudes and weaknesses could play a vital role in the selection of ascetical practices, and the emphasis placed on the practice of the different virtues.

AN INTEGRATED TYPOLOGY

One of the most extensive attempts to create such a differentiated ascetics was made by the Spanish Jesuit Alexander Roldán. Basing himself on William Sheldon's body and temperament types, Roldán attempted to erect corresponding types of holiness, and to illustrate them from the lives of the saints.(2) In view of the probable relationship between Sheldon's work and Jung's typology, Roldán's work could be extended and transformed by being brought into relationship with the attempts currently being made to apply Jung's typology to the spiritual life.(3) If this could be carried out successfully, it would lead to the creation of a much more complete typological instrument suitable for application in spiritual direction. Sheldon extends Jung's type downward to the realm of physical and bio-chemical realities, while Jung brings Sheldon's typology into the psyche itself, and places the emphasis on thera-peutic and developmental questions that Sheldon left in the background.

The refinement of psychological tools to be used in revitalizing the practical science of spiritual direction represents the solution to only one of the two major obstacles to such a renewal. The other must be the strengthening of the life of prayer itself by bringing it into relationship with St. John's writings, even when actual contemplative experience is not in question. The context of mystical experience provides the setting in which the inner nature and impulses towards development of all states of prayer are best examined.

The use of St. John and Jung in the spiritual life is not without dangers. People charged with the office of spiritual directors must be aware of the epistemological problems discussed in Chapter Two, and also resist the temptation to employ this psychological tool in a purely psychological way. Jung's psychology cannot be used to fill the vacuum caused by the impotence of our religious past. Individuation is not identical with spiritual transformation.

From the spiritual side of things an appreciation of St. John of the Cross which has been gaining momentum in recent years poses its own kind of difficulties. Here the temptation is to discover contemplation in many different interior states and in many people where it does not, in fact, exist, and this temptation, far from being a new one, has existed perennially.

BEGINNERS

St. John devoted a fair amount of time to the state of beginners principally because it was the point of departure for the contemplative life. Chapter Three and Four touched on his doctrine, which can be summed up as follows: though this state has an important positive role to play at the beginning of the spiritual life, it is riddled with weaknesses which must be overcome in order to progress. These beginners mistake the strength of their emotions for a depth of spiritual experience.

But is this really a critical contemporary problem for spiritual direction, or simply a phenomenon of the cloister, a fervor of novices that has little to do with the majority of people who practice the life of prayer? Perhaps a brief excursion into the past will give us the necessary perspective to answer this question.

In 1601 and 1607 two works appeared by the Benedictine Leandro de Granada, and the Discalced Carmelite Francisco de Santa María. The first was a Spanish version of the revelations of St. Gertrude with commentary, and the second a separate and expanded version of those commentaries.(4) In these works Leandro and Francisco developed a spirituality in which the obscure loving knowledge of St. John was replaced at the summit of the spiritual life by clear and distinct supernatural apprehensions. These visions and revelations formed a miraculous science of the intellect by which the saints were brought closer to God and enabled to draw great numbers of people to Him. They were, according to our authors, charismatic graces not given simply to the early Church, but throughout its history. It was a mysticism that bases itself on a light higher than faith and led to a kind of intellectual vision. And how were the saints to prepare themselves to receive these high revelations? It was by the practice of contemplation, which can be either affirmative or negative. The negative contemplation leads to a very special grace by which God is known with unspeakable clarity and simplicity, and the soul receives clear and distinct knowledge.

This sounds, of course, like our old friend Thomas of Jesus, and Francisco, in fact, studied with Thomas at

Salamanca and co-founded the Desert of Las Batuecas. His teaching, therefore, can be seen as an "echo of the original teaching that Thomas of Jesus dispensed to the hermits of the reform of St. Teresa".(5)

The crux of the difficulty with this point of view is that it misunderstands what St. John is saying about faith and contemplation. An active negative contemplation, which Thomas patterns on the metaphysical doctrine of the way names are predicated of God, is very different than St. John's negative contemplation which procedes by faith animated by charity. Thomas' negative contemplation goes by simple negation, while St. John's negativity is born out of a positive experience of divine union. Since Thomas' contemplation has no object of fruition and experience, he adds a superstructure to St. John's contemplation in the form of a supereminent degree operating beyond the realm of faith and the gift of wisdom. In this way he attempts to capture the immediacy of mystical experience, never realizing that he has previously emptied it out by transforming St. John's night into the practice of acquired contemplation. Leandro and Francisco cast their own spirituality in a similar mode.

In a basic sense, then, we can define the state of beginners as a state in which the thirst for clear and distinct knowledge is in the forefront. St. John recognized the role that natural apprehensions played in the beginning of the life of prayer, but clear and distinct supernatural kinds of knowledge, far from being an advance over these natural perceptions, still less a culmination of the spiritual life, can be a serious danger to it precisely because they distract the spirit from faith.

If Leandro and Francisco could place this attraction for clear knowledge at the summit of the spiritual life right after St. John's death, it should occasion no surprise if we feel the same inclination to do so today. Whether we have come to the life of prayer from the novitiate or charismatic movement or Cursillo, etc., our beginnings often have much in common because they work through the natural faculties. But the message of St. John is that faith transcends what can be known in this way and can become luminous and experiential. But if the spirit in its thirst for experience focuses on these distinct kinds of knowledge, then it blinds itself to faith and the contemplation that can come through faith.

BEGINNERS AND PSYCHOLOGICAL KNOWLEDGE

If we were to imagine Dr. Jung attending a charismatic prayer meeting or a large assembly gathered for the purpose of healing, we can be sure he would follow the procedings with great interest and respect. He would not be constantly muttering to himself, "Why, this is only psychological", for in his mind the psyche was the very arena through which God acted, and to this extent he would agree with St. John who upheld the important role that this state of beginners played in the economy of the spiritual life. But at the same time he would be sorely puzzled if one of the participants were to tell him that this is the direct working of the Holy Spirit and has nothing to do with the psyche at all. The psychological dimension of things is clear enough in the phenomena of tongue speaking or the procedures followed by large gatherings for the purpose of healing or the dynamics of a Cursillo weekend.

The central issue is, again, the interaction between psychological and spiritual processes. The question is not simply whether God is working, but how is He working. The state of beginners is that of a genuine conversion and true progress in the interior life, but it comes through the medium of the psyche. The psychologist will not be surprised to find that the consolation that St. John talks about employs maternal imagery in describing this state of sensible fervor:

"With no effort on the soul's part, this grace causes it to taste sweet and delectable milk and to experience intense satisfaction in the performance of spiritual exercises, because God is handing the breast of His tender love to the soul, just as if it were a delicate child."(6)

And it is precisely because the life of prayer is working through the psyche that the state of beginners is at once limited and dangerous. St. John would say that the natural working of the faculties is not adequate to attain to union with God, and the beginner is drawn to spiritual exercises as much by the satisfaction as by any purely spiritual motives. For the psychologist, even while he is refraining from making any judgment about the religious object, is often painfully aware that if interior experiences are viewed as if they had nothing to do with the overall dynamics of the psyche, then their recipient runs the risk of damaging his psychic balance. If temptations must be seen only as the direct working of the devil and inspirations and revelations the direct working of the Holy Spirit, then the totality of the psyche and the flow of its energy will be misunderstood.

The biggest danger to the beginner experiencing sensible fervor, or any other tangible phenomenon, is that they will equate their experience purely and simply with union with God. The very combination of genuine spiritual gifts and how these graces work through the psyche creates a sense of conviction that this, indeed, is the work of God, but this conviction is often extended to deny the human dimension as if any participation by the psyche is a denial of divine origin. The beginner, then, can become impervious to psychological and spiritual advice. The sense of consolation, the feeling of completion, the visions seen, or the voices heard, the tongue spoken, or the healings witnessed, are all identified with the exclusive direct action of God as if there were no psyche that received and conditioned these inspirations. This same attitude is then carried over into daily life and how God's action is viewed in this world. If God is so immediately present, miracles must be taking place daily. God must be intervening day-by-day, even in the minor mundane affairs of the recipients of His Spirit. This does not mean that genuine miracles do not take place, nor that genuine inspirations do not play a role in daily life, but rather, if we believe that they are conceptually distinguishable from the ordinary working of consciousness, we run the risk of identifying God's action with our own perceptions, feelings and emotions. The initial conversion state, precisely because of the degree of emotional energy it is charged with, is often clung to as if the intensity of this energy is a guarantee of its spiritual character.

As beginners under the vital force of these tangible experiences we take up an attitude of inner expectancy. We look to a realm beyond the arena of the ego and assume that what transpires there is supernatural. We reach and grasp for interior messages. Thus arises a real danger of misinterpreting what we perceive. What Jung says about the inability to discern between God and the unconscious at the level of empirical experience is verified here. We run the risk of confusing the spiritual with the psychic, our own perceptions with God Himself. An even greater danger is that we will erect this kind of knowledge into a whole theology of the spiritual life, and thus judge our progress by the presence of these phenomena.

The same problem can arise in a completely different context, which could be called a pseudo-Jungian Christianity. In it the realities of the psyche which Jung described are identified with the Christian faith. Thus, at one stroke a vivid sense of experience, even mysticism, if you will, arises. The numinous experience of the unconscious becomes equivalent to the workings of the Holy Spirit. Dreams and the psychological events that take place during the process of individuation are taken for the stages of the life of prayer and the ascent of the soul to God by faith. But this mysticism is no more to be identified with St. John's than the previous one of visions and revelations.

TWO PATHS OF INNER DEVELOPMENT

Even when sensible fervor is not intense, the discernment between psychological and spiritual processes can be vital. If, for example, someone has been converted to the spiritual life, and their devotion to the Blessed Virgin has played an important role in this process, they could very well feel a lively sense of her protection and guidance. This experience of consolation can be developed in two different directions and be the entranceway to two different worlds, for it contains both spiritual and psychological dimensions. The concern of the spiritual director will be to see that these interior feelings lead to the practices of the spiritual life, that is, the exercise of the virtues, mortification, etc., in order that its outcome will be a greater union with God. He will try to help this person to realize that these feelings are not identical with true interior devotion and will probably diminish while the interior devotion to the Blessed Virgin and through her to God can continue to grow. But it would be presumptuous for the spiritual director to deny the repercussions and psychological ramifications of this interior devotion or, while admitting them, ignore the effect they can have on the interior life. From a psychological point of view, the same experience can be seen as a manifestation of the anima, and while the psychologist cannot address himself to the question of whether it has been brought about by some spiritual reality, he can fruitfully explore its nuances which express the actual state of psychic integration. The experience pursued from the point of view of the anima will lead further into the psyche to the underlying archetypal configurations that are connected with it. In this way the psyche conditions the kind of Marian devotion that will appear. The principle danger for the person experiencing this devotion is that as the palpable and sensible feelings diminish, they will seek to prolong them and pursue them irregardless of the direction of genuine spiritual development. They will unconsciously identify psychic aspects with spiritual, and this is detrimental to both psychological and spiritual growth.

THE INTUITION TYPE AND CONTEMPLATION

If the two processes cannot be identified, neither can they be separated as if psyche and soul were two separate realities. An example from a typological point of view can illustrate the difficulties brought about by this kind of separation. The introverted intuition type could be called a natural contemplative. He or she has a special capacity for being attracted by the goal that St. John describes. Their intuition inwardly leaps over any obstacle in a search for their deepest center. They pick up the inner rhythms of St. John's writings and thrill to the idea of letting go of everything in order to reach the supreme goal.

But if we recall the tensions that can develop between spiritual aspirations and the sensible man, these tensions exist in a special way in this type. Their consciousness is dominated by a spiritualizing tendency which wants to avoid extraverted sensation. In practical terms, this can mean difficulties with living in the everyday world of work and family obligations. It can also entail hypersensitivity to sexuality, ambivalence about eating, etc., and out of these problems can arise the provisional life. The intuition is always seeking something better, while unconsciously it is avoiding being pinned down in space and time. Many of the characteristics of what Jungian psychologists have described under the heading of the puer aeternus syndrome are operative here.(7)

These natural tendencies of the introverted intuition type can become suffused with spiritual meanings. Since a person of this type is often at a loss in the world, they can take readily to a conversion process. They can feel that the sacrifices that it entails are not weighty, especially if they hinge on giving up external goods and are in the form of restrictions on worldly activities. All these things have already been undervalued, or negatively valued. In the fervor of conversion this type feels that for the first time they have found their true home, and they expect and hope to fly off into a completely spiritual kingdom where material considerations do not enter. They have only to hear of the mystics and begin to read them to become converted to their way of thinking.

Because the introverted intuition type is using his primary function in order to perceive spiritual values and the innate hierarchy among them, his perceptions can be very valuable. He is exercising a gift he truly possesses. Yet, from a psychological point of view, this tendency to be a spiritual flyer, that is, to be constantly striving to reach a spiritual state of existence, is often coupled with a flight from the unconscious and instinctual realities. The natural inclination of the introverted intuition type to lead a life of prayer can lead to the accumulation of psychic energy around the instinctual centers in the unconscious and produce phenomena similar to those that St. John so carefully describes.

The difficulty in spiritual direction lies in being able to discern the genuine from the spurious on both the spiritual and psychological levels. The director who appreciated the spiritual enthusiasm of this type and neglected the psychological ramifications would be no more adequate than the director who deduces from the psychological difficulties the conclusion that the inner spiritual perceptions are erroneous. Genuine spiritual intuitions can bring in their train unfortunate psychological consequences. The introverted intuition type can fortify himself with an arsenal of theological knowledge and examples and counsels drawn from ascetical and mystical writings. The often genuine insight at the root of his convictions blinds him to the limitations of his position and makes him impervious to advice that appears to be in direct opposition to his conscious position, e.g., get his feet on the ground, find a good job and settle down, etc. This kind of approach is analogous to the psychologist attempting to develop the inferior function directly without the mediation of the second and third functions. However, if the spiritual director can slowly show how the interior attitude of consciousness is producing a counter effect in the form of sensual difficulties, which difficulties are hindering genuine spiritual growth, then he is making an appeal to the strongest motivating force in this kind of personality, which is the desire for spiritual progress. Further, the introverted intuition type has to apply St. John's discussions of the incapacity of sense and intellect, in short, all the natural faculties, to act as proximate means of divine union, to the faculty of intuition itself. His goal is beyond the intuitive faculty despite its natural spiritual and contemplative nature.

Each psychological type possesses its own strengths and weaknesses in living out the spiritual life. The elaboration of detailed descriptions of how these distinctive psychological pathways interact with the stages of the interior life would be the raw material for creating a renewed science of spiritual direction.

CONTEMPLATIVES

We have already seen in Chapter Seven some of the dynamics of psychic energy that surround the beginning of contemplation. The same dual perspective is valuable in understanding the relationship between St. John's teaching about visions and revelations and contemplation. In the **Ascent of Mount Carmel** he devotes a group of chapters to exploring this topic. He starts with an explanation of how even genuine visions can mislead their recipients, and points to the difference between God's interior communication of union and these more palpable phenomena. Then he asks the difficult question, "If we are not to understand or meddle with them, why does God communicate them?" (8) He answers this question as best he can, pointing to various possibilities as, for instance, God's condescension to the weakness of the person involved and the possible intervention of the devil, but his explanations never entirely match the vehemence with which he rejects these things. This is clearly a case where St. John could have used a psychology that would have allowed a choice of origin that was neither God nor devil nor ego.

Karl Rahner developed a fuller explanation of the nature of these visions and why they can mislead and harm the soul. He asserts that the genuine imaginative vision takes place only in the presence of infused contemplation and "is only the radiation and reflex of contemplation in the sphere of the senses, the incarnation of the mystical process of the spirit".(9) Thus, the imaginative vision is only indirectly caused by God as an effect on the psyche of this interior communication.

"If the actual "point" at which God first affects the soul lies deeper, behind the faculties of sense-perception, if it leads primarily to a contact and union of man's spirit with God and thus to the scene of the real work of grace, then it becomes understandable and natural that the echo in man's sensibility of this interior and pivotal process will not be governed exclusively by the process itself, but will also be influenced by all the other dispositions of the visionary which are unconnected with this divine influence, such as elements of fantasy, patterns of perception, selective attitudes of expectation due to religious training, or the historical situation, or aesthetic taste, etc."(10)

Rahner illustrates this process from the lives of the saints who were convinced that they had received a real experience of God and mistakenly extended the certitude of this experience to the visions that it brought forth. If the saints could make this kind of error, it is easier to understand why St. John is so adamant in advising that these kinds of communications be refused. Even if they are refused, the inner grace will be communicated, while if they are accepted, it is very easy to be attracted to their tangible aspects to the detriment of the spiritual.

There are also other possible interactions between psychic processes and contemplative experiences that can become stumbling blocks to further progress. If one temptation of the contemplative at the beginning of this infused prayer is to attempt to continue working with the faculties, another is that having taken up an attitude of receptivity to this new experience, he maintains this attitude even when the contemplation itself disappears. St. John, in the first book of the **Ascent of Mount Carmel**, discusses how meditation and contemplation can be mixed at the beginning of the contemplative life.(11) Thus, the attitude of receptivity to this experience should not be extended when the experience has disappeared. Further, it is not only during the time of prayer when these problems can appear. A contemplative who was actually experiencing the dark night of sense in the strict sense, that is, the actual beginning of contemplation, could, at the same time, be experiencing this dark night mixed with psychological difficulties. If the contemplation is intermittent, then the dark night of sense will diminish, but the psychological problems that were intermixed with it can continue and give the appearance that the dark night itself is still operative, leading the person to maintain a passivity which is no longer warranted.

An accurate delineation of the variety of problems that contemplatives face must be developed from the actual experience of modern contemplatives. The collection of this kind of empirical material would be much more difficult than examining the state of beginners. With the art of spiritual direction in disarray, contemplatives cannot only live in an atmosphere of incomprehension, but they can misunderstand themselves. Yet the actual contemplatives in the Church, no matter how small their number might be, have an important role to play in the re-creation of a better climate for the contemplative life. They hold within themselves the answers to many of the delicate and difficult questions that have to be dealt with in order to develop a renewed science of spiritual direction.

THE NORMALCY OF CONTEMPLATION

Just how normal or common is it to be a contemplative in the explicit sense that St. John gives it? The answer lies in understanding what is meant by normal or ordinary. There can be two very different meanings which can be characterized as essential and existential. From the first point of view contemplation is ordinary and normal in the sense that it flows from the basic structure of the spiritual life. It is a normal flowering of the virtues and the gifts of the Holy Spirit, and this is how St. John and St. Teresa describe it. On the other hand, if we take normal in the existential sense, which means, are people ordinarily and commonly experiencing contemplation as their spiritual lives develop, the answer is probably no. There are many devout people who do not appear to be going by the way of contemplation. In other words, infused contemplation is probably rare.

How can these two different perspectives be reconciled? Perhaps the most developed answer was given by Maritain who, while maintaining that contemplation was the normal development of the life of grace, wanted to avoid two difficulties:

"...that the perfection of charity (even ordinary and common) is reserved to those souls alone who enjoy infused contemplation under its typical and normal form, and if a soul does not arrive at this contemplation which can be called manifest (in its luminous and obscure form) it is always its own fault."(12)

The first part of this solution distinguishes charity from contemplation. The essence of perfection or holiness or union with God is based on love which causes the union and transformation in God that St. John described. Contemplation does not come through the intellect by means of concepts, but it is a knowledge through love. It is the effect, as it were, on the intelligence of the union that already exists through love. It is the expression in terms of knowledge of the love that exists in what the mystics call the center of the soul. Contemplation is an integral part of the life of love without being the essence of it. It is also a tremendous aid in pursuing this union with God because it helps engage the whole personality by giving the person who loves a better understanding of whom they are loving. Even when it is a question of formal canonization, the issue is not the degree of contemplation that has been attained, but the perfection of charity.

If contemplation is an integral and important part of spiritual development, why is it relatively rare? Here we come to the second element in Maritain's answer which deals with the question of generosity. A simple reading of St. John's description of the dark nights suffices to show to what heights self-denial and suffering is carried. Though generosity is a very real problem it would be a mistake to understand it in a completely personal way, that is, a certain individual faced with a clear choice of whether to make the sacrifices necessary to proceed in the contemplative life, refuses. The concrete reality is much more complex. Generosity is linked to knowledge about the spiritual life, and adequate spiritual direction, and the failure to reach contemplation embraces a much wider perspective than simply the interior forum of the individual. Our failures to love are interwoven with the whole fabric of a world that groans for redemption. This fallen-redeemed world that exists both within and outside of us prevents the natural unfolding of the life of charity. Without becoming definitively aware of a decisive moment of choice for or against the contemplative life, and thus for reasons that cannot be ascribed to a want of generosity in a narrow sense, many people are not fitted for the experience of contemplation that St. John describes. The factors that impede contemplation may include both the physical and psychological constitution, upbringing, and even the very vocation they are meant to carry out because this vocation must be carried out in a world that is at odds with the qualities that are necessary for the reception of contemplation. Charity can overcome all obstacles and can increase from moment to moment despite the circumstances of life, but this does not necessarily mean that it will transform the personality in whom it is growing to the degree that is necessary for the experience of contemplation.

Here we enter the mysterious realm of God's actual calls and gifts. In one sense everyone is called to contemplation, since contemplation represents a fore-taste of the life to come. The goal is there to attract us all, and this, in itself, is important because without a clear view of the goal, our own path will be much more obscure. At the same time, it would be a mistake to read St. John in such a way as if he is advocating one path, for this goes against his explicit statements and it can create a rigorism that discourages people from making their own progress in their own way in spiritual life. If we turn St. John's writings into a rigid schema where all the steps are clearly delineated, then we make the assumption that God is calling people the same way, and those who do not progress up the staircase have personally done something that has caused them to fail. This kind of attitude overlooks the legitimate diversities of type, the variety of different gifts in the Church, and the freedom that God has to call people in different ways. A sense of this freedom is extremely important, for without it, people who seriously take up the way of prayer fill their heads with expectations and later with feelings of failure that deflect them from the positive things they can do to progress in the spiritual life.

The very language that St. John uses has an existential sense, that is, it grows out of the concrete situation and deals above all with our inner choices of heart. When he says: "All the being of creation when compared with the infinite being of God is nothing", he is certainly not making an ontological statement that will deny the existence of creatures or the reality of the being they possess. Rather, he is saying all the beings of creation, when desired as if they were greater than the infinite being of God, are nothing, that is, will not get us to our ultimate goal. Yet, even when this is said, there is a deeper sense to this kind of language. We do not live in a world where moral choices are simple and obvious and flow easily as conclusions to rational judgments about what is good and what is better. The dark nights of St. John were his expressions of the fallen state of the world and the need of travelling the way of the Cross. The extreme nature of these nights indicate the degree not of evil as a constitutive or essential element in man's make-up, but of how evil in the form of disordered desires is woven into the very fabric of our world and in the depths of ourselves. The more the life of grace we are called to approaches, the more it shows how unsuited we are to receive it.

The call to contemplation is a call for everyone, yet on the individual level we cannot presume to spell out in advance what this call will look like. We can only try to correspond with the opportunities that actually exist. All the major notions that St. John uses in order to create his view of the life of prayer, that is, contemplation itself, the dark nights, faith as the proximate means of union, are all things that must be applied analogously to each individual situation. To return to Maritain's solution, he distinguishes between people who are in the mystical state where the gifts of the Holy Spirit predominate from those who are not, but among the former, not all are contemplatives in St. John's sense. In some, active gifts predominate so that they do not arrive at the experience of contemplation, or it appears in a masked form, while for others the gift of intelligence and wisdom lead to the contemplative life as St. John has described it. But undoubtedly there are many, many people who, while not being beginners, are not contemplatives and cannot be called contemplatives without radically altering the meaning of the word. Where are they, then?

CHAPTER 9

INBETWEEN

Did St. John actually expect everyone to go by the way of contemplation? In one passage in the **Dark Night** he seems to indicate that there are people who enter the night of sense in the wide sense, that is, fall into aridities, and yet, though they are seriously pursuing the spiritual life, are not meant to arrive at contemplation:

"This night of the aridity of the senses is not so continuous in them, for sometimes they experience the aridities and at other times not, and sometimes they can meditate and at other times they cannot. God places them in this night solely to exercise and humble them, and reform their appetite lest in their spiritual life they foster a harmful attraction toward sweetness. But He does not do so in order to lead them to the life of the spirit, which is contemplation. For God does not bring to contemplation all those who purposely exercise themselves in the way of the spirit, nor even half. Why? He best knows. As a result He never completely weans their senses from the breasts of considerations and discursive meditations, except for some short periods and at certain seasons, as we said."(1)

Unfortunately, since St. John had his mind on contemplation, he never stopped to explore this dimension of the spiritual life, and this omission was to cause difficulties soon after his death.

The creators of the doctrine of acquired contemplation came to grips with this problem but they did so blindly, much like the alchemists struggled with individuation. They were confronted by the dark night in the wide sense, hence their emphasis on the inability to meditate, but infused contemplation did not come to them, and so they attempted to solve the problem in the only way they knew, which was to make themselves into contemplatives.

By inventing an active contemplation they did not find the gold of contemplation, but the problems they grappled with were and still are very real. That is why the problem of active contemplation has never gone away. Let us return for a moment to the history of acquired contemplation to bring the story into the 20th century.

AN ANTI-MYSTICAL ATMOSPHERE

The anti-mystical reactions of the 17th century had become much more damaging when they were amalgamated with a deformation and misunderstanding of the prudential maxims of the saints and spiritual writers.(2) Phrases dealing with the contempt and flight from the world and the dangers of creatures that filled the works of writers on the interior life and which had to be understood in a practical sense, that is, the nothingness of creatures in relationship to our choices for God when we are tempted to choose between the creature and God, were transformed and deformed into a speculative position, not overtly formulated, but covertly accepted. This position created a feeling that creatures were somehow worthless in themselves, that the world and the very earth that God created had to be fled from. This crypto-Manichean attitude remained, as Maritain puts it, an external parasite on the life of piety in the Church for a long time, since the instinctive life, whether understood in a physical, natural sense, or even in a spiritual sense, was too strong and robust and rooted in daily contact with the goodness of the earth and human love to succumb to this error.

Gradually this picture began to change. The infection went deeper and caused a more virulent illness, and reached its culmination during the 19th and early part of the 20th century. Then the prudential maxims of the past assumed enormous proportions because of their ontological pretensions. The flight from the world, ever accentuated by the raw assertions of a world enthralled with its human mastery of events, its scientific achievements and technological marvels which possessed an anti-religious character became a flight from the very foundation upon which a healthy spiritual life should be built.

The asceticism of St. John of the Cross with its practical character and its foundation in the actual contemplative experience was picked up and wielded as a bludgeon by a very different kind of personality. If the door was shut on mysticism, these rigorists attempted to shut it on human nature as well, all under the pretext of avoiding danger, but undoubtedly fed by an external legalistic mentality that saw piety more in the fulfillment of humanly conceived laws and regulations than in the loving submission to a mysterious reality that transcended the limits of any conceptual statement. Men were cut off from their roots below and their roots above. They were urged to flee from their human nature under the pretext not clearly voiced, and therefore all the more insidious, that this nature was completely corrupted by original sin. The thoroughgoing affective and volitional mortification of the mystic for the sake of divine union was degraded into gloomy moral prohibitions that issued from a desiccated theology which was in the process of decay precisely because it had cut itself off from its own sources of life.

Therefore, it became inevitable when at the time of renewal of religious life and theology in the years just after the second Vatican Council that Christians, especially religious, who had borne the brunt of these deficient ideas would find within themselves a tremendous thirst for human things. They would exalt them in the place of what seemed to them the soul-deadening spiritualities under which they had led their lives. They were in no mood to listen to talk about prayer and piety because it was under the guise of such things that this process of dehumanization had wrought its damage. Yet this exaltation of the human could only sustain itself for a limited amount of time, especially when lived out in the world instead of the cloister. What was missing was not simply human, but inner religious experience as well. This was the problem that Jung addressed himself to primarily with people who had lost all living contact with the Christian churches or any living religion, and this is the same problem that still lies at the heart of the renewal of religious life and the life of the Church.

Nothing is harder to recognize the value of than something that has harmed us in a deformed state. The misunderstanding and misues of John of the Cross gave rise to an urge to forget about him and find some new source of inspiration. In actual fact St. John had been rarely read, and even more rarely understood from the positive perspective of actual mystical experience. He evoked a feeling of negation which overburdened people already plagued by doubt and guilt because of their inability to do away with their human nature. The renewal of interest in St. John today has to take into account these undercurrents and misunderstandings that have effected the spiritual life for so long.

ACQUIRED CONTEMPLATION IN THE 20TH CENTURY

Today's interest in mysticism is not simply a post-Vatican II phenomenon. It has its origins at the turn of the century, which was marked by a renaissance of Thomistic studies, and this philosophical and theological renewal embraced the spiritual life as well. Pioneering workers like Juan Arintero and Reginald Garrigou-LaGrange elaborated the theological foundations of the mystical life, while men of a more practical cast of mind like Poulain organized the treasures of the past into practical manuals for nourishing the life of prayer. Yet, despite the value of this work and its wide-spread acceptance, it did not have the impact on the practical order that could have been expected. It had to fight the now deeply entrenched attitude that had dominated the Church since the end of the 17th century. On the practical plane, even in religious communities, mysticism was a matter that was barely discussed, and certainly not proposed as a practical goal and culmination of the spiritual life.

It was perhaps inevitable that a renewed interest in mystical studies would find itself, once again, involved in the problem of acquired contemplation. Abbé Sandreau attacked it as a dangerous innovation, and he was seconded by Lamballe, Juan Arintero and Ignacio Menéndez-Reigada. Père Poulain tried to counter Sandreau's objections, and this by now traditional Carmelite doctrine found champions with the order in men like Claudio de Jesús Crucificado, Crisógono de Jesús, and Gabriel of St. Mary Magdalen. These debates waxed and waned for decades, and are now only remembered by a few scholars, and usually with distaste. Unfortunately, it would be an illusion to believe either the subject matter was, in fact, trivial or some genuine solution had been arrived at after the worst of the partisan fires had died down. The problem of acquired contemplation still exists, and more importantly, the situation out of which it emerged is still being encountered.

Routinely books have appeared throughout this century describing acquired contemplation, attributing it to John of the Cross, and recommending it as a genuine stage in the contemplative life. If there is no genuine doctrine of acquired contemplation, then not only is this energy misdirected, but it tends to obscure the real problems that surround contemplation as a practical possibility today. The problem of acquired contemplation, understood in this wide sense, is like a rhizome that is waiting for the propitious moment to emerge again. The state of the question at the apex of its articulation just before it last faded from view can be seen in Gabriel of St. Mary Magdalen's **Acquired Contemplation** (1946), and the masterly analysis to be found in Roland Dalbiez', **The Controversy of Acquired Contemplation** (1949).

Fr. Gabriel summed up his work in this field as follows:

"After long historical researches in the field of Teresian spirituality, I can safely affirm that the contemplation called by Carmelite theologians acquired or active, is chiefly to be identified with that described by St. John of the Cross, in a form already perfected, in Book II of the **Ascent**, whilst its earliest stage is studied in Book I of the **Dark Night.** Such was the practically unanimous interpretation of the Saint's doctrine during the whole of the first century of the School."(3)

For Fr. Gabriel both acquired and infused contemplation are one from a speculative point of view; they are both caused by the infusion of God. But from a practical point of view they are distinct enough to warrant separate names. Infused contemplation takes possession of the soul completely enough to make itself experimentally felt, while in this other contemplation the divine inflowing is hidden. (4) And the person receiving it is not conscious of it in the same way as infused contemplation, but this hidden contemplation is the cause of its inability to meditate, and so it must now do something else: exercise itself in looking lovingly at God.(5) This active contemplation is much more common and is offered to practically all who are willing to fit themselves for it as they should.(6) In it the intellect no longer reasons discursively, but is content to gaze upon God with a simple loving attention.(7) This loving attention is drawn from the soul by the hidden contemplation.

Fr. Gabriel analyzes the writings of St. John and St. Teresa in this light. For the most part St. Teresa has limited herself to describing this experimental infused contemplation, while St. John knows of another kind of contemplation in which God doesn't make Himself felt, and which can fittingly be called common or ordinary or active or acquired contemplation. He provides us with a story of a young cleric who is making the transition from meditation to contemplation. First he is full of enthusiasm and fervor, and his meditations go well, and before too much time passes, they begin to simplify themselves into loving colloquies filled with affective aspirations. "But, one fine day, lo and behold, the whole scene is changed!"(8) He finds no sweetness in his prayer. He cannot meditate. His director mistakenly puts it down to insufficient preparation, or punishment for a past sin, or simply recommends patience in affliction. In Fr. Gabriel's mind, St. John of the Cross would have given very different advice. He would tell the young student that he need not meditate, but on the positive side he must exercise himself in a general and loving attention to God who is present.(9) Since this infusion remains hidden, "the Saint gives three signs whereby this may be identified."(10)

"There is a sufficiently lengthy period of time in contemplative prayer during which the divine action remains hidden."(11) Acquired contemplation, then, is an "intermediate state between affective meditation and contemplation properly infused."(12) Instead of feeling the divine action, "the soul **feels nothing** of the divine action"; "It must become aware that God is really working in it. Therefore, it needs special guidance to enable it to identify the hidden operation which has begun."(13) It must not hinder this inner operation but "maintain itself in the best disposition for receiving it."(14) And this is done by practicing loving attention. The director must encourage the person who is trying to maintain himself in this state because "as this state is sometimes prolonged for years the soul, even if used to lovingly attending to God, has at times the impression of being 'in a void'."(15)

In summary, in this state of acquired contemplation, "the soul has indeed something to do albeit its activity is very simple. It must do nothing but look lovingly upon its God with the gaze of faith. It is not to make reflections; it is not to form distinct concepts; the time for such has gone by. It must now remain in His company and content itself with being simply and lovingly aware of His presence."(16) "The soul 'practices', it 'exercises itself' in the simple, loving gazing upon God."(17) This loving activity is a general attention to God. "The infused divine light is not felt" and "the soul is conscious only of its own activity, of its simple and loving attention to God."(18) While active contemplation is expounded by Fr. Gabriel with a certain flair and smoothness, it is essentially the same as that of Thomas of Jesus, and labors under the same problems.

Roland Dalbiez' study begins with an analysis of the Carmelite mystical theologian Joseph of the Holy Spirit, who died in 1736, and was recognized as one of the most profound scholastic thinkers in the field of mysticism. Dalbiez turns this scholastic language to good account by carefully examining the meaning of acquired contemplation in Joseph's **Cursus Theologiae Mystico-Scholasticae**. He finds that there is a contradiction: Joseph states that in some places this contemplation is acquired, and in other places that it is not, and Fr. Joseph asserts it is a contemplation, and then turns around and asserts it is not. Then Dalbiez turns to the broader question of whether the whole idea of acquired contemplation can be maintained. There are four possibilities, each of which can be represented by a historical figure:

"The first is that of the radical quietist, the prototype of which is Molinos. The second is that of the mitigated or semi-quietist, which is represented by Fénelon. The third is that of the Catholic theologians for which the degree of prayer called acquired contemplation is only improperly acquired, and this position is found fully elaborated in Scaramelli. The fourth, no less orthodox, is that of the authors in the eyes of which acquired contemplation is only a contemplation improperly speaking, this is the conception of St. Alfonsus Liguori."(19)

The first and second possibilities lead to theological unorthodoxy, while the third and fourth remain orthodox by emptying acquired contemplation of its proper meaning. The notion of acquired contemplation from a historical point of view leads to difficulties, not only because it cannot be found in St. John, but because the advocates of this doctrine in the 17th century seem to slide into difficulties maintaining it. As Dalbiez puts it: "It is the notion of acquired contemplation which has created the psychological climate without which the blossoming of quietism would have been impossible."(20) Dalbiez, after stating the historical case against acquired contemplation with devastating clarity, and this at a meeting organized by the Carmelites, attempted to provide a formula of reconciliation:

"Metaphysically, there is but one contemplation, which is infused. Psychologically, there are two contemplations, one whose infused character is conscious for the subject, and one whose infused character is unconscious for the subject."(21)

He remarks that it would be a mistake to conclude that since all contemplation is "ontologically passive" it is "consciously passive", that is, actually experienced as passive infused prayer. This notion deserves particular attention because it represents the most developed attempt at resolving the controversy. It drew the following response from Fr. Gabriel:

"This last part of the position of M. Dalbiez constitutes precisely the thesis we have defended for a long time in our book **Acquired Contemplation**...We cannot but applaud this aspect of M. Dalbiez' work."(22)

Are we, then, confronted with a genuine solution to this long-standing problem? Unfortunately not. It is certainly true that St. John describes a time of transition in which infused contemplation has not yet become conscious, but we cannot conclude that this description coincides with the state described by the advocates of acquired contemplation. Dalbiez has based his attempt at bridge building by indicating "the ontological unity and the empirical duality"(23) of contemplation, but the crux of the difficulty is whether the state described by St. John and the state described by the proponents of acquired contemplation are the same. If they are not, then we are dealing with a real empirical duality that is based on two very different states.

A PSYCHOLOGICAL DARK NIGHT

The foundation for discerning these two different states depends on a careful reading of St. John's three signs. The dark night was used by St. John in both a wide and narrow sense. In the wide sense it meant that recollected people fell into aridities, and this is how the proponents of acquired contemplation understood it. But the three signs are meant to define the dark night of sense in a strict way as the actual beginning of contemplation. The first two signs are not enough: the third must be present, for only the third differentiates between infused contemplation and various psychological counterparts:

"When one is incapable of making discursive meditation upon the things of God and disinclined to consider subjects extraneous to God, the cause could be melancholia or some other kind of humor in the heart or brain capable of producing a certain stupefaction and suspension of the sense faculties. This anomaly would be the explanation for want of thought or of desire and inclination for thought." (24)

Melancholy, the black bile of the ancients which they thought gave birth to depression, was part of this psychological vocabulary that St. John had to work with. Even though this vocabulary was rudimentary from a modern point of view, it might have contained a greater degree of insight than we can recapture today. Baruzi, for example, suggests that John might have come in contact with one of the noted physicians of the time, Gómez Pereira, while he was working in the hospital in Medina del Campo. One of the works of this learned doctor was entitled, **Concerning the Fevers Arising from Melancholy and the Signs of Them.**(25) Victor White makes the astute observation that melancholy could be associated with the introverted intuition type.(26)

Melancholy could not only counterfeit the dark night, but when it was a question of the unruly movements of sense during the time of prayer, it could magnify these difficulties:

"These impure thoughts so effect people who are afflicted with melancholia that one should have great pity for them; indeed, they suffer a sad life. In some who are troubled with this bad humor the trial reaches such a point that the devil, they think, definitely has access to them without their having the freedom to prevent it; yet some of these melancholiacs are able through intense effort and struggle to forestall this power of the devil.

If these impure thoughts and feelings arise from melancholia, a person is not ordinarily freed from them until he is cured of that humor, unless the dark night flows in

upon the soul and deprives it successively of all things."
(27)

Thus, both melancholy and the true contemplative night of sense could be operative in the same person, and this same point is made again later in the **Dark Night:**

"There is thus a great difference between aridity and lukewarmness, for lukewarmness consists in great weakness and remissness in the will and in the spirit, without solicitude as to serving God; whereas purgative aridity is ordinarily accompanied by solicitude, with care and grief as I say, because the soul is not serving God. And, although this may sometimes be increased by melancholy or some other humour (as it frequently is), it fails not for that reason to produce a purgative effect upon the desire, since the desire is deprived of all pleasure, and has its care centered upon God alone. For, when mere humour is the cause, it spends itself in displeasure and ruin of the physical nature, and there are none of those desires to serve God which belong to purgative aridity."(28)

These comments of St. John on melancholy which played an important role in his formulation of the doctrine of the three signs appear to have been lost sight of by the men who formulated the doctrine of acquired contemplation. Perhaps the vocabulary was inadequate to transfer the genuine insights contained under this heading, or spiritual directors were looking for a specific morbid disposition and did not find any signs of it in these recollected people they were guiding. In any event, these comments of St. John can form the basis for developing a fuller psychological explanation of the plight of the people who have arrived at the first two signs and cannot find in themselves any experience of contemplation.

Melancholy in a more general sense can be understood as a lack of conscious energy available to the ego that gives rise to feelings of depression and dead-endedness. St. John in his descriptions of beginners in the spiritual life emphasizes the energy they have to devote themselves to spiritual activities and the corresponding sense of consolation and fulfillment they feel as a result of them. To use a water analogy of the kind St. John and St. Teresa favored, the beginner is using his bucket, and finding water wherever he drops it. Even though this water is being scooped up by the natural working of the faculties, it is so readily available that it forms a sensible analogate to what takes place in contemplation itself. From a psychological point of view, energy is available to the ego and it utilizes it to broaden its perspective.

Recollected people ply their bucket more assiduously than others, but since they are actually drawing up this water and expending it, the day arrives when the level of the water falls below the length of the rope that holds their bucket. This same phenomenon can be viewed from the point of view of the development of the various functions and attitudes in the process of individuation. The natural working of the faculties can then be understood as the use of the most conscious or superior function with its attendant attitude, aided by the auxiliary function. The conscious exercise of these functions, especially when it is deliberate and cultivated, can lead to the same dilemma of lack of conscious energy. What development that could have taken place through these functions has already been substantially achieved. There is no more psychic energy that can be attained through exercising them. What is needed is a new function through which to tap a deeper level of energy. Dr. Jung and his followers carefully fashioned various ways in which this new function, and thus new ways of proceding, and new energy could be developed.

For St. John, the most favorable prognosis for this diminishment of conscious energy would be the dawning of the experience of contemplation, and thus he gives the three signs for determining whether this is actually the case, but the three signs imply that there are other explanations possible, as we have just seen.

Both Jung and John in their own ways are leading the person caught in this predicament of energylessness to a positive new experience, to a new source of energy, and this is how they differ from the proponents of acquired contemplation. When the recollected person comes up dry, he needs to either add a length of rope to his bucket by a process of psychological development or arrive at other ways of watering the garden by contemplation. But when he is given the advice to practice acquired contemplation, he is being told to exercise his natural faculties with ever greater subtlety, and somehow by this exercise of loving attentiveness attain to the actual experience of contemplation. This procedure tends only to exhaust the last reaches of psychic energy available to the faculties and pave the way by which psychic energy from the unconscious will burst into the vacuum being created in consciousness. From this point of view it is not at all surprising that a position of acquired contemplation, pushed to its extreme, in, for example, the quietism of Molinos, could give rise to powerful sensual movement that appeared to the recipient as autonomous actions of the devil.

Loving attentiveness is one thing when the inability to meditate is a result of the actual beginning of contemplation, but it is quite another when it is a question not of a new spring of water welling up in the center of the soul, but simply the more general psychological fact that the conscious working of the faculties cannot reach down to the level of the water. To take up an attitude of loving attentiveness in the latter situation is to expect the water to jump up into the bucket. Men cannot live in a vacuum freed from actual experience. Even in realms of faith and prayer there is a need of experience, though the form it might take can be quite different from everyday ones. St. John with all his emphasis on mortification never suggested trying to live in a void. As he puts it:

"For, in order to conquer all the desires and to deny itself the pleasures which it has in everything, and for which its love and affection are wont to enkindle the will that it may enjoy them, it would need to experience another and a greater enkindling by another and a better love, which is that of its Spouse."(29)

If we return to the case of Fr. Gabriel's young cleric, throughout the discussion of the possible reasons for his inability to meditate, the question of melancholy, depression or temperament never comes up. If this dark night has not been brought about due to some kind of lack of diligence or recent imperfection, this does not mean that the only alternative left is that it must be the dark night of contemplation. It could be a natural diminishment of conscious psychic energy due precisely to the diligence with which he attended to his spiritual exercises. In this case exercising loving attentiveness, while it feels like you are in a void, will only diminish further the energy the ego has available and hasten the possibility of an antagonistic outburst from the unconscious.

And antagonism is not the only possible response that the unconscious can make. In the passage that describes the necessity of the third sign and talks of humours that can cause "a certain stupefaction and suspension of the sense faculties", and thus leave a person without thought or the desire for thought, St. John concludes in a strange fashion:

"(The humour) would foster in a person the desire to remain in that delightful ravishment."(30)

There is nothing in the immediate context that explains what "that delightful ravishment" is, but perhaps St. John expected that his readers in the Order of Mount Carmel would understand, for it recalls passages in St. Teresa. For example, in the **Interior Castle** she described the counterfeit of true inner experience:

"When they experience any spiritual consolation, therefore, their physical nature is too much for them; and as soon as they feel any interior joy there comes over them a physical weakness and languor, and they fall in a sleep, which they call "spiritual", and which is a little more marked than the condition that has been described. Thinking the one state to be the same as the other, they abandon themselves to this absorption, and the more they relax, the more complete becomes this absorption, because their physical nature continues to grow weaker. So they get it into their heads that it is **arrobamiento,** or rapture. But I call it **abobamiento,** foolishness; for they are doing nothing but wasting their time at it and ruining their health."(31)

Nor would this "delightful ravishment" have been a mystery to Jung. The energizing of the unconscious that can result from the suspension of conscious activity can have a pleasant aspect so that the ego, instead of fleeing, is tempted to rest in the embrace of this experience. This is especially true if the recipient confuses this delightful ravishment with contemplation itself. The passivity needed for the reception of contemplation will become a passivity which is an abdication of the necessary standpoint of the ego. The ego that gives up its own perogatives and submerges itself in the unconscious, and the ego which flees the unconscious and thus evokes counter tendencies both illustrate the underlying dynamics of the psyche that are a foundation of the life of prayer. Did some of the proponents of acquired contemplation experience this inner delight and confuse it with contemplation? Juan Falconi, for example, in his **Straight Road,** states that during contemplation:

"thou art as if ravished (embelesado), as if in darkness, so that thou knowest not what thou doest or doest not, and even thinkest that thou wilt perish."(32)

This attitude of receptivity will in the absence of contemplation easily be transformed into a receptivity that will become aware of the contents in the unconscious which have attained almost enough energy in order to become conscious. If for someone like Molinos they have a sexual nature, then he will begin to create spiritual explanations, i.e., the devil wishes to stop the practice of this contemplation.

By calling this a psychological dark night I am trying to point out its continuity with other developmental problems where energylessness and the search for a new attitude play major roles. From this point of view this dark night is a call to psychological growth. The functions that were engaged in the life of prayer can no longer work as they did before, but if the psyche can be developed, new energy will be available to employ in praying.

But we are at a delicate point. To imply that psychological development is the total answer would obscure the fact that we are dealing with the spiritual life, while to talk in a purely spiritual language like the active contemplatives is to miss the very real and important psychological dimension.

Both these directions must be taken into account if we are to arrive at a viable solution. We can hardly say that we can no longer employ the natural faculties if, in fact, there is a whole dimension of the psyche which could become conscious and add an important breadth to these faculties. Individuation is a much more comprehensive way of judging what belongs to the natural psyche, and thus to what St. John calls meditation. I have looked at this developmental problem elsewhere from a typological point of view, and there is abundant literature on individuation. (33) It is the other half of the question that is much less talked about.

THE WAY OF FAITH

This is the need to pray actively despite the dark nights. The energy that is derived from pursuing this process of psychological development can be utilized in the exercise of the spiritual life, but even with new energy available there is no guarantee that the satisfaction and sensible consolation that existed in spiritual exercises before the darkness set in will be rediscovered. In fact, things will probably be quite different. There is a natural process of simplification in ordinary prayer which once experienced is not likely to be reversed. One of the positive benefits that came out of the long saga of acquired contemplation was a heightened appreciation of the variety of states that comprised the prayer that St. John labeled meditation. Methodical discursive meditation which culminates in an affective conclusion leads to a situation where the affective part of the prayer predominates, and this, in its turn, can simplify so that the principle affect is one of love, and the principle object God, Himself. The guiding thread in this process of simplification is the following of the water of consolation and satisfaction. We do what seems to draw us closer to the spiritual goal of union with God, and simplification is but the concentration on the means that seem the most effective for reaching this goal.

Acquired contemplation is mistaken, not because it delineated this process of simplification, but rather, because it misunderstood the nature of contemplation. It thought that taking up an attitude of expectancy with the natural faculties, a loving attentiveness, would be the best disposition for receiving contemplation, but the natural working of the faculties, no matter how passively we exercise them, which, of course, tends to be a contradiction, cannot attain contemplation because contemplation does not come through the faculties.

Not only will this new stage of prayer be simplified, but it will be without sensible consolation, and yet, if it is not the beginning of contemplation, it is a prayer that must be prayed. It is an active exercise of the faculties, even though in a simplified manner. There are no simple apprehensions or intuitions that can be maintained more than a few seconds as the culminating leap of the discursive process, nor are there any enduring acts that by-pass the need to actively exercise mind and heart in order to pray. The ordinary practices of the active spiritual life have to be maintained, that is, the conscientious practice of the various virtues, mortification, the Sacraments and spiritual reading, etc. Since sensible consolation has evaporated, faith comes to the forefront, the faith that St.

John calls the only proximate means of union with God, that is a faith working through charity that can be lived out without sensible consolation, without contemplative experience, and without trying to constantly make it into the receptivity of an experience that is not there.

This faith has as many opportunities to grow as there are moments that can be given to prayer, chances to put more love into our relationships with others and problems and trials that must be borne. It can nourish itself on St. John's writings on the goal of the spiritual life and on the detachment that faith demands, aware that he is talking about the gift of contemplation but also realizing that this active exercise of faith is the best preparation for whatever gifts God has in store for us.

If we are not beginners and not contemplatives, we can still be men and women of faith. And this is not a blind faith, for it works through love and guides us so that we can say with St. John:

"I went without discerning
And with no other light
Except for that which in my heart was burning."(34)

EPILOGUE

MAGNUM OPUS

There has been a certain amount of progress in meeting the three initial challenges that stood in the way of using St. John and Jung in the spiritual life.

I have tried to steer a middle course between what Marie-Louise Von Franz has called the old king, that is, a theology so jealous of its perogatives as to be closed to the insights of psychology, and a facilely conceived Jungian spirituality that would identify the archetypes with the Christian mysteries. Christian spirituality is in dire need of the kind of help Jungian psychology can give, but to profit from it, it has to appreciate the differences in methods and goals that exist.

Further, it has to clarify its own history. This means rediscovering St. John, clearing away the incrustations of past misinterpretations, and delving into the shamefully neglected field of modern spirituality from the 17th through the 20th century. The question of acquired contemplation is only one of the issues at stake, but it illustrates how far some spiritual writers have strayed from St. John, and it is particularly significant because Jung's psychology allows us to pose an alternative solution to the problem of the inability to meditate.

Yet, neither epistemology nor history will be of any avail if Christian spirituality loses sight of the overriding practical issue involved, which is the restoration of the life of prayer under the twin lights of individuation and contemplation. Hopefully, the discussions in Part III have given us a glimpse of the possibilities that exist in this direction.

A TASK FOR THE FUTURE

But to follow this path calls for a collaboration between Jungian psychology and Christian spirituality, and such a joint effort, while difficult, would not have been foreign to Jung's mind. He wrote in his first letter to Victor White, "...I would surely be among the first to welcome an explicit attempt to integrate the findings of psychology into the ecclesiastical doctrine." And later, at the time of Fr. White's death, "I had nursed the apparently vain hope that Fr. Victor would carry on the magnum opus." Strange and powerful words. What is the magnum opus but a renewal of the religious life of the West? Christian spirituality and Jung's psychology, despite their differences, share this ultimate intent, and this is the most basic foundation for their collaboration. This common work could be carried out by Jungian analysts, theologians of the spiritual life, and people devoted to the life of prayer, especially contemplatives by gift and by state of life. Then the discussions initiated by Jung and Fr. White so many years ago at Bollingen would finally bear fruit.

NOTES

CHAPTER 1.
1. Memories, Dreams, Reflections, p. 355.
2. Excellent introductory material is available on Jung's psychology, e.g., Jung, ed., Man and His Symbols and Mattoon, Jungian Psychology in Perspective.
3. Memories. p. 13.
4. Ibid., p. 17.
5. Ibid., p. 36.
6. Ibid., p. 39.
7. Ibid., p. 42.
8. Ibid., p. 72.
9. Ibid., p. 62.
10. Ibid., p. 93.
11. Ibid., p. 109.
12. Ibid., p. 194.
13. Ibid., p. 196.
14. Ibid., p. 205.

CHAPTER 2.
1. Jung, Collected Works, Vol. 8, p. 109.
2. Bash, Introduction to General Clinical Psychopathology, p. 50.
3. Heisig, Imago Dei, p. 108.
4. Jung as cited in Jaffe, The Myth of Meaning, p. 30.
5. On this issue see Raymond Hostie, Religion and the Psychology of Jung, and the response of Victor White, Critical Notice on Hostie.
6. Memories, p. 351.
7. Ibid., p. 351.
8. Ibid., p. 337.
9. Ibid., p. 94.
10. Ibid., p. 337.
11. Ibid., p. 351-2.
12. Ibid., p. 43.
13. Collected Works, Vol. 11, p. 580.
14. Jaffe, The Myth of Meaning, Chapter 4.
15. Maritain, Preface to Metaphysics.
16. The Degrees of Knowledge, p. 149.
17. A Tool for Understanding Human Differences, Ch. 7.
18. C.W., 6, p. 527.
19. The Degrees of Knowledge, p. 192.
20. Maritain, Philosophy of Nature, p. 162.
21. Ibid., p. 88.
22. The Degrees of Knowledge, p. 65.
23. Philosophy of Nature, p. 111.
24. Memories, p. 221. "In dem Augenblick, wo ich den Boden erreichte, stieß ich gleichzeitig an die äußerste Grenze des mir wissenschaftlich Erfaßbaren, an das Transzendente, das Wesen des Archetypus an sich, worüber sich keine wissenschaftlichen Aussagen mehr machen lassen."
25. Cunningham, Victor White and C.G. Jung.
26. Letters, Vol. 1, p. 383.

27. Letters, Vol. 1, p. 385.   28. Ibid., p. 387.
29. Ibid., p. 448.   30. Ibid., p. 448 N 1.
31. Ibid., p. 448.   32. Ibid., p. 449.   33. Ibid., p. 501.
34. Ibid., p. 501.   35. Letters, Vol. 1, p. 540-1.
36. Ibid., p. 540-1.   37. Ibid., p. 555.   38. Ibid., p. 555.
39. Ibid., p. 486.   40. Ibid., p. 487.   41. Ibid., p. 487.
42. Letters, Vol. 2, p. 72.   43. Ibid., p. 73.
44. Ibid., p. 228.   45. Cunningham, p. 324.
46. Ibid., p. 324.   47. Letters, Vol. 2, p. 536.

CHAPTER 3.
1. Ascent, Prologue, No. 7, p. 72, Kavanaugh and Rodriguez translation (KR).
2. Ascent, Book 1, Chapter 3, No. 3, pp. 76-7, KR.
3. Ascent, 1,4,3, p. 78, KR.
4. Ascent, 1,4,1, p. 77, KR.
5. Dark Night, 1,1,2, p. 298, KR.
6. Ascent, 1,14,2, p. 105, KR.
7. Ascent, 2,13,1, p. 140, KR.
8. Ascent, 2,5,7, p. 117, KR.
9. Ascent, 2,4,2, p. 113, KR.
10. Ascent, 2,3,4, p. 111, KR.
11. Dark Night, 1,9,8, p. 315, KR.
12. Living Flame of Love, Stanza 3, 32, p. 622, KR.
13. Dark Night, 1,8,3, p. 312, KR.
14. Ascent, 2,13,4, p. 141, KR.
15. Ascent, 2,13,7, p. 141, KR.
16. Ascent, 2,14,6, p. 144, KR.
17. Dark Night, 1,9,6, pp. 66-7, Peers translation.
18. Living Flame, S 3, 34, p. 622-3, KR.
19. Dark Night, 1,10,4, p. 317, KR.

CHAPTER 4.
1. An extensive bibliography can be found in B.A.C. edition of the Obras Completas de San Juan de la Cruz.
2. Ascent, 2,12,3, p. 128, Peers (P).
3. Ascent, 2,12,4, p. 128, P.
4. Ascent, 2,12,5, p. 129, P.
5. Ascent, 2,14,1, p. 136, P.
6. Ascent, 2,14,8, p. 141, P.
7. Ascent, 2,14,8, p. 141, P.
8. Ascent, 2,14,10, p. 142, P.
9. Dark Night, 1,9,8, p. 67-8, P.
10. Ascent, 2,12,6, p. 130, P.
11. Ascent, 2,12,7, p. 131, P.

12. Ascent, 2,13,7, p. 136, P.
13. Ascent, 2,14,4, p. 138, P.
14. Ascent, 2,14,6, p. 139, P.
15. Ascent, 2,14,6, p. 139, P.
16. Ascent, 2,14,10, p. 142, P.
17. Ascent, 2,15,3, p. 149, P.
18. Ascent, 2,15,3, p. 150, P.
19. Dark Night, 1,10,1, p. 69, P.
20. Dark Night, 1,10,6, p. 72, P.
21. Dark Night, 1,12,1, p. 76, P.
22. Dark Night, 1,14,1, p. 88, P.
23. Living Flame, S 3, 30, p. 103, P.
24. Living Flame, S 3, 34, p. 108, P.
25. Living Flame, S 3, 42, p. 113, P.
26. Ascent, 2,12,6, p. 130-1, P.
27. Dark Night, 1,10,1, p. 69, P.
28. Dark Night, 1,14,1, p. 88, P.
29. Living Flame, S 3, 31, p. 103, P.
30. Living Flame, S 3, 30, p. 103, P.
31. Living Flame, S 3, 42, p. 113, P.
32. Ascent, 2,12,8, p. 132, P.
33. Ascent, 2,12,8, p. 132, P.
34. Ascent, 2,13,7, p. 135, P.
35. Ascent, 2,13,7, p. 136, P.
36. Ascent, 2,15,5, p. 150, P.
37. Ascent, 2,15,5, p. 150, P.
38. Dark Night, 1,9,3, p. 64, P.
39. Dark Night, 1,9,4, p. 65, P.
40. Dark Night, 1,9,6, p. 66, P.
41. Dark Night, 1,9,6, p. 66, P.
42. Ascent, 2,14,8, p. 141, P.
43. Ascent, 2,14,10, p. 143, P.
44. Ascent, 2,14,12, p. 145, P.
45. Ascent, 2,14,12, p. 146, P.
46. Dark Night, 1,10,4, p. 71, P.
47. Dark Night, 1,10,4, p. 317, KR.
48. Ascent, 2,14,2, p. 137, P.
49. Ascent, 2,14,2, p. 138, P.
50. Ascent, 2,14,6, p. 139-40, P.
51. Living Flame, S 3, 32, p. 104, P.
52. Living Flame, S 3, 32, p. 105-6, P.
53. Living Flame, S 3, 31, p. 103-4, P.
54. Ascent, 2,13,4, p. 134, P.

CHAPTER 5.
1. **Memories**, p. 203.
2. **Gloria y Ocaso**, Part 2, p. 420.
3. Ibid., p. 420. Yet the attribution to St. John started very early. In 1618 there was a manuscript of the **Tratado Breve** bearing the name of Fray Juan de la Cruz. (Gerardo, **Obras de Místico Doctor**, p. 271.)
4. **Studies of the Spanish Mystics**, Vol. 2, Tomás de Jesús, p. 219ff.
5. **Ascent**, ixvii, Peers.
6. Peers, **Studies of the Spanish Mystics**, Vol. 2, p. 223.
7. Simeon, **Un Nuevo Códice Manuscrito** and **Tomás de Jesús y San Juan de la Cruz** for Thomas' citation of St. John.
8. I am indebted to Jean Krynen's Le "Cantique Spirituel"... at many points in my evaluation of Thomas of Jesus. Krynen's work has not gotten the attention it deserves. His assertion that Thomas of Jesus rewrote St. John's **Spiritual Canticle** is just one element in a wider synthesis that attempts to give a historical explanation for the differences between the doctrine of John of the Cross and the spirituality of the beginning of the 1600s. The story of acquired contemplation is another dimension of this same riddle, and starting from different preoccupations it, too, leads back to the fertile pen of Thomas of Jesus.
9. A detailed analysis can be found in Peers (note 4) and José de Jesús Crucificado, **El P. Tomás de Jesús, Escritor Místico.**
10. **Tomás de Jesús y S. Juan de la Cruz**, p. 139.
11. Simeon, **Contenido Doctrinal**, p. 68.
12. Ibid., p. 74.
13. Ibid., p. 77-8.
14. (Thomas of Jesus) **Tratado Breve**, p. 312-13.
15. Simeon, **Tomás de Jesús y San Juan de la Cruz**, p. 153.
16. Peers, **Studies of the Spanish Mystics**, Vol. 2, p. 238.
17. **De Contemplatione Acquisita**, p. 63.
18. Krynen, **Le Cantique Spirituel**, p. 318, note 2.
19. Simeon, **Un Nuevo Codice Manuscrito**, p. 133-4.
20. **Dark Night**, 1,9,6, p. 66, P.
21. **Dark Night**, 1,10,4, p. 317, KR.
22. Maritain, **Sur l'appel a la vie mystique.** Also his remarks on philosophical contemplation in **Pas de savoir**

sans intuitivité, p. 411ff, in **Approches Sans Entraves.**
23. Ascent, 2,14,11, p. 145, P. Peers also gives the readings from the first edition.
24. Ascent, 2,15,2, p. 149, P.
25. Living Flame, S 3, 31, p. 103, P.
26. Living Flame, S 3, 46, p. 117, P.
27. Dark Night, 1,9,9, p. 68-9, P.
28. Living Flame, S 3, 31, p. 104, P.
29. Living Flame, S 3, 32, p. 105-6, P.
30. Dark Night, 1,9,6, p. 66, P.
31. Dark Night, 1,10,5, p. 71, P.
32. Ascent, 2,12,8, p. 132, P.
33. Krynen shows a possible divergence between Quiroga and the spirituality of the deserts in **Saint Jean de la Croix, Antolinez et Thomas de Jesus.**
34. **Don que Tuvo,** p. 534.
35. Baruzi, **Saint Jean de la Croix et le Problème de l'expérience mystique,** p. 710-11.
36. Peers, **The Complete Works,** Vol. 3, p. 384.
37. Optat de Veghel, **Benoit de Canfield,** p. 478ff.
38. Pacho, **San Juan de la Cruz y Juan de Santo Tomás.**
39. Ibid., p. 357.   40. Ibid., p. 382-3.
41. Gomez, **Estudios Falconianos.**
42. Peers, **Studies of the Spanish Mystics,** Vol. 2, p. 285.
43. Gomez, p. 82.
44. Peers, **Studies,** Vol. 2, p. 286.
45. Ibid., p. 287.   46. Ibid., p. 296.
47. Ibid., p. 301.
48. Baker, **The Confessions,** p. xxvii.
49. Baker, **Contemplative Prayer,** p. 358.
50. Ibid., p. 359.   51. Ibid., p. 365.   52. Ibid., p. 361.
53. Knowles, "Fr. Augustine Baker" in **The English Mystical Tradition.**
54. Baker, **Confessions,** p. 169.
55. Molinos, **The Spiritual Guide,** p. 55. On Molinos cf. Knox and Dudon.
56. Ibid., p. 59.   57. Ibid., p. 60.   58. Ibid., p. 64-5.
59. Ibid., p. 72.
60. Eulogio, "El Quietismo..." on these parallels and **La Defensa de la Contemplación.**
61. Knox, **Enthusiasm,** p. 312.
62. This is the opinion we can draw from the explicit testimony of Thomas of Jesus, Knowles on Fr. Baker, Eulogio on Molinos, and the cases of Falconi and Rojas

point in the same direction.

63. There are other threads of this tapestry that remain unexplored. In 1689 an anonymous Jesuit, writing after Palafox had published a **Carta Pastoral** on the condemnation of Molinos, denied the existence of acquired contemplation and said that maintaining that position would make St. John a Molinosista (Crisógono, **San Juan de la Cruz, su obra científica**, p. 184).

Dudon makes Quiroga the unwitting inspirer of Petrucci, that episcopal companion of Molinos (cf. Claudio, **Cuestiones Místicas**, p. 67).

There is also the case of Antonio Panes and his **Escala Mística** (1675). Did Panes draw from some of the same sources as Molinos (cf. Robres and Martin) and if so, how did he escape condemnation and have his book republished in 1743?

CHAPTER 6.

1. The factual data can be found in the biography of Crisógono de Jesús (in **Vida y Obras de San Juan de la Cruz**, revised and augmented by Matias del Niño Jesús) and a penetrating portrait of St. John in Brenan, **St. John of the Cross**, with poems translated by Lynda Nicholson.

2. Cf. Arraj and Arraj, **A Tool...**, Chapter 2.

3. Holmes, "A Jungian Approach to Forgetting and Memory in St. John of the Cross", in Sullivan (Ed.), **Carmelite Studies II**, p. 178ff.

4. Gomez-Menor, **El Linaje Familiar...**

5. Brenan, p. 33.

6. Sheldon, **Psychotic Patterns and Physical Constitution,** p. 865.

7. Brenan, p. 5.	11. Ibid., p. 18.	15. Ibid., p. 127.
8. Ibid., p. 8.	12. Ibid., p. 32.	16. Ibid., p. 116.
9. Ibid., Ch. 2.	13. Ibid., p. 36.	17. Ibid., p. 153.
10. Ibid., p. 23.	14. Ibid., p. 53.	

18. **Spiritual Canticle**, Prologue, No. 1, p. 408, KR.

CHAPTER 7.

1. Jung, **Collected Works**, Vol. 6, p. 419.

2. **C.W.** 8, p. 18.   3. Ibid., p. 12.

4. **Dark Night**, 1,4,1, p. 303, KR. This passage was one of the topics in a defense in 1618 by Basilio Ponce de León to save St. John's writings from condemnation. Fray Basilio comments:

"Let not the spiritual man, then, be forthwith discouraged and afflicted and let him not suppose that his state of prayer is of the devil. It may be of God and yet this may happen, either because of some natural effect that is caused **ex accidenti** in the body, through weakness or heat or dilation of the pores, or through the inspiration of the devil, who, since he cannot enter the loftiest place of contemplation, is anxious to cause such disturbances as he can. And sometimes these things will come to pass not only without any desire on the part of the contemplative, but even without his perception or knowledge, as happens in dreams, because the force with which the spiritual man is bound closely to his contemplation will not permit him to have knowledge of these movements or of any other exterior actions...Our author does not say that these sensual motions arise immediately or **per se** from the spirit of the contemplation of God. He says that, at the time when the soul is conscious of the pleasure of contemplation, some sensual delight is wont to be felt in weak natures, and that this delight has its natural explanation in philosophy and medicine. For overmuch joy heats the body and dilates the pores, just as fear makes the body cold and closes the pores. And thus what this author postulates is an effect of the weakness of the body and not of the grace and spirit of contemplation...

"In this author, however, I find them described as sensual motions not caused by the spirit, whereas in the Illuminists I find grossness described as being an effect of the spirit." (Peers, **The Complete Works of St. John of the Cross**, Vol. III, p. 418-20.) For two modern cases see Von der Heydt.

5. **Dark Night**, 1,4, p. 303-6, KR.

6. Ibid.	9. Ibid.	12. Ibid.
7. Ibid.	10. Ibid.	13. Ibid.
8. Ibid.	11. Ibid.	14. Ibid.

15. **Dark Night**, 1,4,3, p. 49, P.
16. **Dark Night**, 1,8,3, p. 62, P.   17. Ibid.
18. **Dark Night**, 1,13,3, p. 83, P.
19. **Dark Night**, 1,13,15, p. 87, P.
20. **Living Flame**, S 3, 54, p. 122-3, P.
21. **Ascent**, 2,11,10, p. 135, KR.   22. Ibid.
23. **Living Flame**, S 3, 55, p. 123-4. P.
24. **Dark Night**, 1,14,1, p. 88, P.
25. **Dark Night**, 1,14,2, p. 88, P.

26. Dark Night, 1,14,3, p. 88-9, P.
27. Dark Night and comments by Fordham, The Dark Night of the Soul.
28. Letters, Vol. 2, p. 159.
29. Dark Night, 1,4,3, p. 308, KR.

CHAPTER 8.
1. The Degrees of Knowledge, p. 314.
2. Roldán, Personality Types and Holiness.
3. On Jungian typology and the spiritual life, cf. Grant, Kelsey, Michael and Norrisey; on integrating Sheldon and Jung, cf. Arraj and Arraj, A Tool for Understanding Human Differences.
4. Krynen, Du Nouveau sur Thomas de Jesus.
5. Ibid., p. 129.
6. Dark Night, 1,1,2, p. 298, KR.
7. Von Franz, Puer Aeternus.
8. Ascent, 2,20,6, p. 171, KR.
9. Rahner, Visions and Prophecies, p. 57.
10. Ibid., p. 62-3.
11. Ascent, Ch. 21.
12. Maritain, Sur l'appel a la vie mystique, p. 73 and p. 81, note 1.

CHAPTER 9.
1. Dark Night, 1,9,9, p. 316, KR.
2. Maritain, The Peasant of the Garonne, p. 44-50.
3. Gabriel, Acquired Contemplation, p. 92.
4. Ibid., p. 94.
5. Ibid., p. 93.
6. Ibid., p. 94.
7. Ibid., p. 101.
8. Ibid., p. 116.
9. Ibid., p. 119.
10. Ibid., p. 120.
11. Ibid., p. 121.
12. Ibid., p. 121.
13. Ibid., p. 121.
14. Ibid., p. 121-2.
15. Ibid., p. 122.
16. Ibid., p. 142.
17. Ibid., p. 143.
18. Ibid., p. 149.
19. Dalbiez, La Controverse de la Contemplation Acquise, p. 109.
20. Ibid., p. 117.
21. Ibid., p. 132.
22. Ibid., p. 77.
23. Ibid., p. 133.
24. Ascent, 2,13,6, p. 141, KR.
25. Baruzi, p. 80, note 3.
26. White, God and the Unconscious, p. 127.
27. Dark Night, 1,4,3, p. 304-5, KR.
28. Dark Night, 1,9,3, p. 64-5, P.
29. Ascent, 1,14,2, p. 73, P.
30. Ascent, 2,13,6, p. 141, KR.

31. Teresa of Avila, **Interior Castle,** p. 92-3.

32. Peers, **Studies of the Spanish Mystics,** p. 297.

33. cf. Arraj and Arraj, **A Tool for Understanding Human Differences,** Part II; for actual cases of individuation, cf. Adler, **The Living Symbol,** and Jacobi, **Symbols in an Individual Analysis;** in Jung (ed.), **Man and His Symbols;** for stages of adult development, Levinson, **The Seasons of a Man's Life.**

34. "En una noche oscura", Campbell, p. 27.

BIBLIOGRAPHY

Adler, G. (1961). The Living Symbol. A Case Study in the Process of Individuation. New York: Pantheon Books, Inc.

Allard, Jean-Louis. (1981). "Maritain's Epistemology of Modern Science. A Summary Presentation." In Conference-Seminar on Jacques Maritain's The Degrees of Knowledge. Saint Louis: American Maritain Association, pp. 144-69.

Arraj, Tyra and Arraj, Jim. (1985). A Tool for Understanding Human Differences. How to Discover and Develop Your Type According to Dr. C.G. Jung and Dr. William Sheldon. Chiloquin, Oregon: Tools for Inner Growth.

Baker, Fr. Augustine. (1907). Contemplative Prayer. Ven. Father Augustine Baker's Teaching Thereon: From 'Holy Wisdom'. Edited by Dom B. Weld-Blundell. New York: Benziger Brothers.

_____ (1922). The Confessions of Venerable Father Augustine Baker, O.S.B., extracted from a Manuscript Treatise preserved in the Library of Ampleforth Abbey, and Edited by Dom Justin McCann, Monk of Ampleforth. New York: Benziger Brothers.

Baruzi, J. (1924). Saint Jean de la Croix et le problème de l'expérience mystique. Paris: Librairie Felix Alcan.

Bash, K.W. (1961). Introduction to General Clinical Psychopathology. Zurich: C.G. Jung Institute.

Basilio Ponce de León. (1622). "Reply of R.P.M. Fray Basilio Ponce de León." in The Complete Works of St. John of the Cross, Vol. III. (1949). Translated and Edited by E. Allison Peers. Westminster, Maryland: The Newman Press. pp. 382-434.

Baudouin, Charles. (1957). "Le symbole chez saint Jean de la Croix." Psychoanalise du symbole religieux. Paris: Librairie Fayard. pp. 234-67.

Brenan, Gerald. (1973). St. John of the Cross. His Life and Poetry. With a translation of his poetry by Lynda Nicholson. Cambridge: University Printing House.

Burrell, David B., C.S.C. (1974). Exercises in Religious Understanding. Notre Dame, London: Uni. of Notre Dame Press.

Claudio de Jesús Crucificado, O.C.D. "Cuestiones místicas.

Relaciones de la Escuela de Tomás de Jesús con el Quietismo." **Monte Carmelo,** Vol. XXVI, pp. 66-75.

_____"Verdadera Doctrina de N.V.P. Tomás de Jesús sobre Contemplación Adquirada". **Mensajero de Santa Teresa,** vol. ii. pp. 378-82, 429-33, 461-6, Vol. iii, pp. 13-18, 54-61, 83-90, 172-77, 219-24, 254-8.

Cognet, Louis. (1959). **Post-Reformation Spirituality.** New York: Hawthorn Books. (The 41st volume of the 20th century Encyclopedia of Catholicism.)

_____(1966). **La Spiritualité Moderne. 1. L'essor:** 1500-1650. Aubier, pp. 176-86.

Crisógono de Jesús Sacramentado, P. (1929). **San Juan de la Cruz, su obra científica y su obra literaria.** (Two volumes). Avila.

_____(1972). Matias del Niño Jesús, O.C.D. and Lucinio Ruano, O.C.D. **Vida y Obra de San Juan de la Cruz.** Madrid: Biblioteca de Autores Cristianos. 6th edition.

Cunningham, Adrian. (1981). "Victor White and C.G. Jung. The Fateful Encounter of the White Raven and the Gnostic." **New Blackfriars,** Vol. 62, Nos. 733/734, July/August 1981, pp. 320-34.

Dalbiez, R. (1938). "Marie-Thérèse Noblet, considérée du Point de Vue Psychologique". In **Etudes Carmélitaines** xxiii, pp. 210-34.

_____(1949). "La Controverse de la Contemplation Acquise." In **Technique et Contemplation. Etudes Carmélitaines.** Desclée de Brouwer, pp. 81-145.

Doran, Robert M., S.J. (1979). "Jungian Psychology and Christian Spirituality." Part I, II, and III in **Review for Religious,** July, pp. 497-510; Sept., pp. 742-52; Nov., pp. 857-66.

Dudon, P. Père. (1921). **Le Quietiste espagnol Michel Molinos.** Paris: Gabriel Beauchesne.

Duvivier, Roger. (1971). "Annexe 3 D'une Edition Avortée a L'Action Missionaire" in **La Genèse Du "Cantique Spirituel" de Saint Jean de la Croix.** Paris: Société d'Edition "Les Belles Lettres".

Egan, Keith J., O. Carm. (1975). "The Prospects of the Contemporary Mystical Movement: A Critique of Mystical Theology." **Review for Religious,** Vol. 34, No. 6, Nov., pp. 901-10.

Eulogio de la V. del Carmen, O.C.D.(1962). "El Quietismo Frente al Magisterio Sanjuanista sobre la Contemplación." Ephemerides Carmeliticae, Vol. 13, pp. 353-426.

_____(1968). Introducción a San Juan de la Cruz. El Hombre, Los Escritos, el Sistema. Madrid: Edit. Católica, Biblioteca de Autores Cristianos.

_____(1968). "San Juan de la Cruz". Ephemerides Carmeliticae. Roma: Teresianum.

_____(1969). San Juan de la Cruz y sus escritos. Madrid: Ediciones Cristiandad.

Ferraro, Joseph.(1976). San Juan de la Cruz y el Problema místico. "La necesidad de un nuevo concilio." Puebla: Impresa en los Talleres Rotográficos de Editorial.

Fordham, Michael. (1958). "Analytical Psychology and Religious Experience", pp. 113-29. "The Dark Night of the Soul", pp. 130-48. "Repression and Christian Practices", pp. 149-67. In The Objective Psyche. London: Routledge and Kegan Paul.

_____(1973). "The empirical foundation and theories of the self in Jung's works." In Analytical Psychology: A Modern Science. The Library of Analytical Psychology, Vol. 1. London: William Heinemann Medical Books Ltd.

Gabriel of St. Mary Magdalen, Fr. (1946). "St. John of the Cross and the Modern Mystical Problem", pp. 91-9. "Acquired Contemplation", pp. 100-202. In St. John of the Cross. Doctor of Divine Love and Contemplation. Maryland: The Newman Bookshop.

_____(1953). "Ecole Mystique Thérésienne (Carmes Déchaussés)", pp. 171-90, 207-10. In Dictionnaire de Spiritualité; Ascetique et mystique; Doctrine et histoire. Parie: Beauchesne.

Gomez Dominguez, Elias. (1965). Estudios Falconianos Dos Cartas Historicas. Madrid: Publicaciones del Monasterio de Poyo.

Gomez-Menor Fuentes, José. (1970). El Linaje Familiar de Santa Teresa y de San Juan de la Cruz. Salamanca, Spain: Gráficas Cervantes, S.A.

Grant, W. Harold, Thompson, Magdala and Clarke, Thomas E. (1983). From Image to Likeness. A Jungian Path in the Gospel Journey. New York: Paulist Press.

Greeff, Dr. Etienne de. (1938). "Succédanés et concomitances psychopatologiques de la "Nuit obscure" (Le cas du Père Surin: 1600-65). In Etud. Carmel. 23,2, pp. 152-72.

Green, Fr. Thomas H., S.J. (1979). When the Well Runs

Dry. Notre Dame, Indiana: Ave Maria Press.

Hardy, Richard. (1982). **Search for Nothing. The Life of John of the Cross.**

Heisig, James W. (1973). "Jung and Theology: A Bibliographical Essay." In **Spring: An Annual of Archetypal Psychology and Jungian Thought.** New York. pp. 204ff.

_____(1979). **Imago Dei, A Study of C.G. Jung's Psychology of Religion.** Cranbury, NJ: Associated University Presses.

Holmes, Russell. "A Jungian Approach to Forgetting and Memory in St. John of the Cross", in Sullivan (Ed.) **Carmelite Studies II: Contemporary Psychology and Carmel.** Washington: ICS.

Hostie, Raymond, S.J. (1957). **Religion and the Psychology of Jung.** New York: Sheed & Ward.

Howley, John. (1920). **Psychology and Mystical Experience.** St. Louis, MO: B. Herder Book Company.

Jaffe, Aniela. (1971). **The Myth of Meaning.** New York: C.G. Jung Foundation/Putnam.

John of the Cross, St. **The Collected Works of St. John of the Cross.** Translated by Kieran Kavanaugh, O.C.D. and Otilio Rodriguez, O.C.D. (1964). New York: Doubleday & Company, Inc.

_____**Ascent of Mount Carmel.** Translated and edited by E. Allison Peers. (1958). Garden City, NY: Image Books.

_____**Dark Night of the Soul.** Translated and edited by E. Allison Peers. (1959). Garden City, NY: Image Books.

_____**Spiritual Canticle.** Translated and edited by E. Allison Peers. (1961). Garden City, NY: Image Books.

_____**Living Flame of Love.** Translated and edited by E. Allison Peers. (1962). Garden City, NY: Image Books.

_____**St. John of the Cross Poems.** With a translation by Roy Campbell. (1960). Baltimore: Penguin Books.

_____ **The Complete Works of St. John of the Cross.** 3 Volumes. (1949). Translated and edited by E. Allison Peers. Westminster, MD: The Newman Press.

_____**Vida y Obras de San Juan de la Cruz.** 6th Edition. (1972). Madrid: Biblioteca de Autores Cristianos. Contains the biography by Crisógono de Jesús,

O.C.D., revised and augmented by Matias del Niño Jesús, O.C.D., edited by Lucinio Ruano, O.C.D.

_____ San Juan de la Cruz. Obras Completas.(1982). 11th Edition. Edited by Lucinio Ruano de la Iglesia. Madrid: Biblioteca de Autores Cristianos.

_____ Obras del Místico Doctor San Juan de la Cruz. 3 Volumes. Edición crítica. (1912). Edited by Gerardo de San Juan de la Cruz. Toledo.

José de Jesús Crucificado, O.C.D. (1949). "El P. Tomás de Jesús, Escritor Místico." In Ephemerides Carm., 3 (1949) and Ephem. Carm., 4 (1950).

Jung, C.G. (1959). "Psychological Aspects of the Mother Archetype." In Coll. Works, Vol. 9, Part I: Archetypes and the Collective Unconscious. New York: Bollingen Series XX.

_____ (1961). Memories, Dreams, Reflections. New York: Vintage Books.

_____ (1964). Man and His Symbols. New York: Dell Publishing.

_____ (1969). "The Significance of Constitution and Heredity in Psychology" in The Structure and Dynamics of the Psyche. Coll. Works, Vol. 8. Princeton, NJ: Princeton University Press. Bollingen Series XX, pp. 107-113.

_____ (1969). The Structure and Dynamics of the Psyche. Coll. Works, 8. Princeton, NJ: Princeton University Press.

_____ (1969). Psychology and Religion: West and East. Coll. Works, 11. Princeton, NJ: Princeton University Press.

_____ (1970). Aion. Researches into the Phenomenology of the Self. Coll. Works, 9, II. Princeton, NJ: Princeton University Press.

_____ (1970). Mysterium Coniunctionis. Coll. Works, 14. Princeton, NJ: Princeton University Press.

_____ (1971). Psychological Types. Coll. Works, 6. Princeton, NJ: Princeton University Press.

_____ Letters, Vol. 1: 1906-1950, and Vol. 2: 1951-1961. Princeton, NJ: Princeton University Press.

Kelsey, Morton T. (1982). "Psychological Types and the Religious Way." in Christo-Psychology. New York: Crossroad, pp. 68-90.

Kilduff, Fr. Thomas, O.C.D. (1980). "Spiritual Direction and Personality Types." in Spiritual Life, Vol. 26, No.

3, Fall 1980, pp. 149-58.

Knowles, David. **The English Mystical Tradition.** New York: Harper & Brothers.

Knox, R.A. (1950). **Enthusiasm. A Chapter in the History of Religion.** London: Oxford University Press.

Krynen, Jean. (1948). Le **"Cantique Spirituel"** de Saint Jean de la Croix, Commente et Refondu au XVIIe Siecle. Un Regard Sur L'Histoire de L'Exegese du Cantique de Jean. Filosofía y Letras, Tomo III. Universidad de Salamanca.

_____(1951). "Saint Jean de la Croix, Antolínez et Thomas de Jésus". in **Bulletin Hispanique,** 53, pp. 393-412.

_____(1962). "Du Nouveau sur Thomas de Jésus" in **Bulletin Hispanique,** 64 bis, pp. 113-35.

_____(1963). "Aperçus sur le Baroque et la Theologie Spirituelle". in **Baroque de Montauban,** pp. 27-35.

Laigne-Lavastine, P. (1937). "Concomitance des états pathologiques et des "trois Signes"." in **Etud. Carmel.,** pp. 154-62.

Lea, Henry Charles, L.L.D. **Chapters from the Religious History of Spain Connected with the Inquisition.** New York: Burt Franklin.

Levinson, Daniel, et.al. (1978). **The Seasons of a Man's Life.** New York: Knopf.

Lhermitte, Jean. (1937). "Etude biologique des états d'aridité mystique." in **Etud. Carm.,** pp. 99-101.

Mager, Dom A. (Oct. 1938). "Le fondement psychologique de la purification passive." in **Etud. Carm.,** pp. 240-53.

Mallory, Marilyn May. (1977). **Christian Mysticism: Transcending Techniques.** Amsterdam: Van Gorcum, Assen.

Maritain, Jacques and Raissa. (1924). "Sur l'appel a la vie mystique et a la contemplation." in **De la vie d'oraison.** Paris: Louis Rouart et fils, pp. 72-95.

Maritain, Jacques. (1951). **Philosophy of Nature.** To which is added Maritain's Philosophy of the Sciences by Yves R. Simon. New York: Philosophical Library.

_____(1953). **Creative Intuition in Art and Poetry.** New York: Meridian Books, The World Publishing Co.

_____(1959).**The Degrees of Knowledge.** New York: Charles Scribner's Sons.

_____(1962). **A Preface to Metaphysics.** New York: Mentor Omega Books.

_____**Approches Sans Entraves.** Paris: Fayard.

_____(1968). The Peasant of the Garonne. New York: Holt, Rinehart and Winston.

Maritain, Raissa, (1974). Raissa's Journal. Presented by Jacques Maritain. Albany, NY: Magi Books, Inc.

Martin, Melquiades Andres. (1975). Los Recogidos. Nueva Visión de la Mística Española (1500-1700). Madrid: Fundación Universitaria Española.

Mattoon, Mary Ann. (1981). Jungian Psychology in Perspective. New York: The Free Press.

Michael, Chester P. and Norrisey, Marie C. (1984). Prayer and Temperament. Charlottesville, VA: Open Door.

Molinos, Miguel de. The Spiritual Guide. London: Methuen & Co., Ltd., 1950.

Moreno, Antonio, O.P. (1978). "Contemplation According to Teresa and John of the Cross". in Review for Religious, Vol. 37, 1978/2, pp. 256-67.

Neumann, Erich. (1968). "Mystical Man". in The Mystic Vision, Papers from The Eranos Yearbook, Bollingen Series XXX 6, Princeton Uni. Press, pp. 375-415.

Optat de Veghel, O.F.M. Cap. (1949). Benoit de Canfield (1562-1610). Sa Vie, sa doctrine et son influence. Romae: Institutum Historicum Ord. Fr. Min. Cap.

Orcibal, Jean. (1966). Saint Jean de la Croix et les mystiques rheno-flamands. Desclée de Brouwer.

Pacho, Eulogio. (1971). "San Juan de la Cruz y Juan de Santo Tomás, O.P. En El Proceso Inquisitorial Contra Antonio de Rojas". in Eph. Carm. 22, pp. 349-90.

Panes, Fr. Antonio. (1743). Escala Mística y Estímulo de Amor Divino. Valencia: Por Geronimo Conejos.

Peers, E. Allison. (1960). Studies of the Spanish Mystics. Three Volumes. London: S.P.C.K.

Poulain, A., S.J. (1957). The Graces of Interior Prayer. A Treatise on Mystical Theology. London: Routledge & Kegan Paul Limited.

Pourrat, Rev. Pierre. (1953). Christian Spirituality. Three Volumes. Maryland: The Newman Press.

Quiroga, Padre Fray José de Jesús María, O.C.D. "Don que tuvo San Juan de la Cruz para guiar las almas a Dios". in Obras del Místico Doctor San Juan de la Cruz. Edición Crítica by Gerardo de San Juan de la Cruz. (1912). Toledo. Three volumes.

Rahner, Karl. (1963). Visions and Prophecies. New York: Herder & Herder.

Repicky, Robert A., C.S.B. (1981). "Jungian Typology and

Christian Spirituality". in **Review for Religious,** Vol. 40, 1981/3. May/Jung 1981, pp. 422-33.

Robres Lluch, Ramón. (1971). "En torno a Miguel de Molinos y los origenes de su doctrina. Aspectos de la piedad barroca en Valencia (1578-1691)" in **Anthologica Annua,** 18, pp. 353-463.

Rohrbach, Peter-Thomas,O.C.D. (1966). **Journey to Carith. The Story of the Carmelite Order.** Garden City, NY: Doubleday & Co., Inc.

Roldán, Alexander, S.J. (1968). **Personality Types and Holiness.** Staten Island, NY: Alba House.

_____**San Ignacio de Loyola a la Luz de la Tipología.**

Ruiz, Federico, O.C.D. (1968). **Introducción a San Juan de la Cruz. El hombre, los escritos, el sistema.** Madrid: Biblioteca de Autores Cristianos.

Sanford, John A. (1971). "Analytical Psychology: Science or Religion? An Exploration of the Epistemology of Analytical Psychology" in **The Well-Tended Tree: Essays into the Spirit of our Times,** edited by Hilde Kirsch. New York: G.P. Putnam's Sons, pp. 90-105.

Saudreau, Auguste. (1924). **The Mystical State. Its Nature and Phases.** New York: Benziger Brothers.

Sheldon, W.H. (with the collaboration of Stevens, S.S. and Tucker, W.B.) (1940). **The Varieties of Human Physique: An Introduction to Constitutional Psychology.** New York: Harper.

Sheldon, W.H. (with the collaboration of Stevens, S.S.) (1942). **The Varieties of Temperament: A Psychology of Constitutional Differences.** New York: Harper.

Sheldon, W.H., Lewis, N.D.C. and Tenney, A.M. (1969). "Psychotic Patterns and Physical Constitution: A Thirty-Year Follow-Up of Thirty-Eight Hundred Psychiatric Patients in New York State". in **Schizophrenia: Current Concepts and Research.** (ed. D.V. Siva Sankar). New York: PJD Publications, pp. 838-912.

Simeon de la Sgda. Familia, O.C.D. (1950). "La Obra Fundamental del P. Tomás de Jesús, Inedita y Desconocida". in **Eph. Carm.,** 4, pp. 431-518.

_____(1950). "Un Nuevo Códice Manuscrito de las Obras de San Juan de la Cruz, Usado y Anotado por el P. Tomás de Jesús". in **Eph. Carm.,** 4, pp. 95-148.

_____(1952). "Contenido doctrinal de la Primera Parte del Camino Espiritual de Oración y Contemplación." in El Monte Carmelo, 60, pp. 3-36, 145-72, 233-52.

_____(1955). "Tomás de Jesús y San Juan de la Cruz", in Eph. Carm., 5 (1951-54), pp. 91-159.

_____(1961). "Gloria y Ocaso de un Apócrifo Sanjuanista. El Tratado Breve del Conocimiento Oscuro de Dios Afirmativo y Negativo". in El Monte Carmelo, 69, pp. 185-208, 419-40.

Smith, Robert C. (1977). "Empirical Science and Value Assumptions: Lessons from C.G. Jung", in Journal of Religion and Health, Vol. 16, No. 2, pp. 102-9.

Sullivan, John, editor. Carmelite Studies I: Spiritual Direction. Washington: ICS.

_____Carmelite Studies II: Contemporary Psychology and Carmel. Washington: ICS.

Sumner, Oswald. (1948). St. John of the Cross and Modern Psychology. London: Guild of Pastoral Psychology, Lecture No. 57.

Teresa of Avila, St. Interior Castle. Translated and edited by E. Allison Peers. (1961). Garden City, NY: Image Books.

Thomas of Jesus. "El Tratado del conocimiento oscuro de Dios afirmativo y negativo y modo de unirse con Dios por amor." in Obras del Místico Doctor San Juan de la Cruz. Edición Crítica. (1912). Edited by Gerardo de San Juan de la Cruz. Toledo. Three volumes.

Thomas a Jesu, Ven. P., O.C.D. (1922). De Contemplatione Acquisita. Tipografía S. Lega Eucaristica. Milano. pp. 43-141.

Trouble et Lumière. (1949). Les Etudes Carmelitaines. Desclée de Brouwer.

Von der Heydt, Vera. (1970-72). "The Treatment of Catholic Patients." in Jour. of Analytical Psychology, pp. 72-80.

Von Franz, Marie-Louise.(1970) Puer Aeternus. New York: Spring Publications.

_____(1974). Number and Time. Northwest University Press.

_____(1975). C.G. Jung: His Myth in Our Time. New York: C.G. Jung Foundation.

Welch, John, O. Carm. (1982). Spiritual Pilgrims. Carl Jung and Teresa of Avila. New York: Paulist Press.

White, Victor, O.P. (1955). "Jung on Job", in Blackfriars, March, pp. 52-60.

_____(1958). "Critical Notice on Hostie". in **Jour.** of Analytical Psychology 3, pp. 97-101.

_____(1961). **God and the Unconscious.** Cleveland: Meridian Books.

_____(1960). **Soul and Psyche. An Enquiry into the Relationship of Psychotherapy and Religion.** London: Collins.

INDEX

THE TREASURES OF SIMPLE LIVING

A FAMILY'S SEARCH FOR A SIMPLER AND MORE MEANINGFUL LIFE IN THE MIDDLE OF A FOREST

by TYRA ARRAJ with JAMES ARRAJ

Our future was set out for us: full-time jobs, mortgage payments for the next 20 years, and retirement at 65. Our children would go to school and we would see them as much as our busy schedules allowed. But such a future held no attraction for us. So we packed up, left it all behind and drove into the unknown.

Our journey took us beyond the electric lines, telephone, paved roads and television. We built our own house, grew salads year-round in a solar greenhouse and taught our children at home, all in the midst of a forest where the nearest neighbors are wild animals and the snow gets four feet deep.

The inconveniences were soon forgotten in the joys of living under our own roof, watching our children blossom, and discovering abilities we never knew we had. The simplicity took away economic pressures and gave us time to search for life's deeper meanings.

PART I explains why we left the city, how we solved the problem of earning a living, and what we went through once we bought a piece of land in the middle of a forest. Read about: the rat race, searching for land, house-building, alternative utilities, a greenhouse-bioshelter, tofu and tempeh, life without a television, and home school.

PART II tells about the treasures we found in our simple life, why our experiment paid us back a thousandfold, and the dream of a bioshelter community.

PART III describes common obstacles to creating a new lifestyle closer to nature, and some important skills like crafts, economic basics, orthomolecular medicine, and the study of human differences, that helped us along the way.

PART IV is a **Resource Guide** for those who might like to begin their own adventure in simple living, including books and organizations on the subjects covered in the first three sections.

FROM THE INTRODUCTION

216 pages, 5 1/2 x 8 1/2, paperback,
resource guide, 14 line drawings, index
ISBN 0-914073-04-4, $11.95.

The Treasures of Simple Living "is engrossing reading - a new Swiss Family Robinson in the late 20th Century!"
Catholic Sentinel

"An idyllic but passionately challenging account of transition from middle-class, city turmoil to taking personal control..."
Learning Unlimited Network of Oregon

A JUNGIAN PSYCHOLOGY RESOURCE GUIDE

Compiled by Tyra Arraj and James Arraj

This unique reference work to Jungian Psychology today describes:

Local and Professional Groups in the United States and Canada
Local and Professional Groups Around the World
Psychological Types Organizations
Conferences
Periodicals
Book Publishers
Mail Order Book Sources
Libraries and Bibliographical Tools
Basic Reading List and Films
Jungian Analysis and Training Programs

It shows you where to find the answers to:
Who was C.G. Jung? What did he say? How can I get
a real picture of what he was like? How can I get an idea
of books and articles that exist about Jung's psychology?
Where can I get books on Jungian psychology? Where do
I look when starting research on a topic in Jungian psychology? Where can I find a Jungian analyst? Where can
I meet people interested in Jung? What periodicals exist
in Jungian psychology or with Jungian-oriented material?
What is Jungian Analysis like? How can I find the up-to-
date programs of U.S. local and professional groups? How
can I keep track of the activities of foreign professional
groups?

144 pages, paperback, index, $11.95.
ISBN 0-914073-05-2

TRACKING THE ELUSIVE HUMAN

VOLUME I
A Practical Guide to
C.G. Jung's Psychological Types,
W.H. Sheldon's Body and
Temperament Types
and Their Integration

by Tyra Arraj and James Arraj

VOLUME I gives clear descriptions of C.G. Jung's eight
psychological types, and the body and temperament types
of William Sheldon, interwoven with an actual account of
what it is like to go on the inner journey of individuation
by way of typology. These typologies are. seen in their true
light as practical ways of dealing with daily life. It treats
of type recognition, type development, and how types play
a role in falling in love, marriage, and bringing up children. It puts special emphasis on the crucial role of our
fourth or least developed function. The descriptions are
enlivened by line drawings, cartoons and self-discovery
quizzes.

Start on the trail that leads to the discovery of your own type and its development. Here is a compassionate and tolerant view of what makes people different that will serve you well both at home and on the job.

184 pages, paperback, index, $11.95
ISBN 0-914073-16-8

ORDER FORM

Please send me:

Quantity	Title	Price
_____	St. John of the Cross and Dr. C.G. Jung	$11.95
_____	The Treasures of Simple Living	$11.95
_____	A Jungian Psychology Resource Guide	$11.95
_____	Tracking the Elusive Human, Vol. I	$11.95

Add $1.00 for the first book and $.50 for each additional book. Enclosed is my check/money order for $_____

NAME_____

STREET_____

CITY_____STATE_____ZIP_____

Send to: INNER GROWTH BOOKS
           Box 520
           Chiloquin, OR 97624

ORDER FORM

Please send me:

Quantity	Title	Price
_____	St. John of the Cross and Dr. C.G. Jung	$11.95
_____	The Treasures of Simple Living	$11.95
_____	A Jungian Psychology Resource Guide	$11.95
_____	Tracking the Elusive Human, Vol. I	$11.95

Add $1.00 for the first book and $.50 for each additional book. Enclosed is my check/money order for $_____

NAME_____

STREET_____

CITY_____STATE_____ZIP_____

Send to: INNER GROWTH BOOKS
           Box 520
           Chiloquin, OR 97624

ORDER FORM

Please send me:

Quantity	Title	Price
_____	St. John of the Cross and Dr. C.G. Jung	$11.95
_____	The Treasures of Simple Living	$11.95
_____	A Jungian Psychology Resource Guide	$11.95
_____	Tracking the Elusive Human, Vol. I	$11.95

Add $1.00 for the first book and $.50 for each additional book. Enclosed is my check/money order for $_____

NAME_____

STREET_____

CITY_____STATE_____ZIP_____

Send to: INNER GROWTH BOOKS
          Box 520
          Chiloquin, OR 97624

ORDER FORM

Please send me:

Quantity	Title	Price
_____	St. John of the Cross and Dr. C.G. Jung	$11.95
_____	The Treasures of Simple Living	$11.95
_____	A Jungian Psychology Resource Guide	$11.95
_____	Tracking the Elusive Human, Vol. I	$11.95

Add $1.00 for the first book and $.50 for each additional book. Enclosed is my check/money order for $_____

NAME_____

STREET_____

CITY_____STATE_____ZIP_____

Send to: INNER GROWTH BOOKS
          Box 520
          Chiloquin, OR 97624

ABOUT THE AUTHOR

Jim Arraj lives with his wife and children deep in a forest far from paved roads and power lines near Crater Lake, Oregon. There they built their own house, grow vegetables in a solar greenhouse, survive 4 feet of snow in the winter and write books about simple living, Jungian psychology, philosophy and religion.

St. John of the Cross and Dr. C.G. Jung "is concerned with finding a synthesis between the writings of St. John of the Cross and the psychology of C.G. Jung as an inspiration to the life of prayer."

The Journal of Analytical Psychology

"John of the Cross and Jung were both concerned with the cure of souls; both lived through profound, painful experiences that qualify them to engage in that enterprise...The story of Jung's encounter with Fr. White suggests the difficulties of a task which nevertheless must be carried out: the collaboration of psychology and theology."

Choice